The Literary Cat

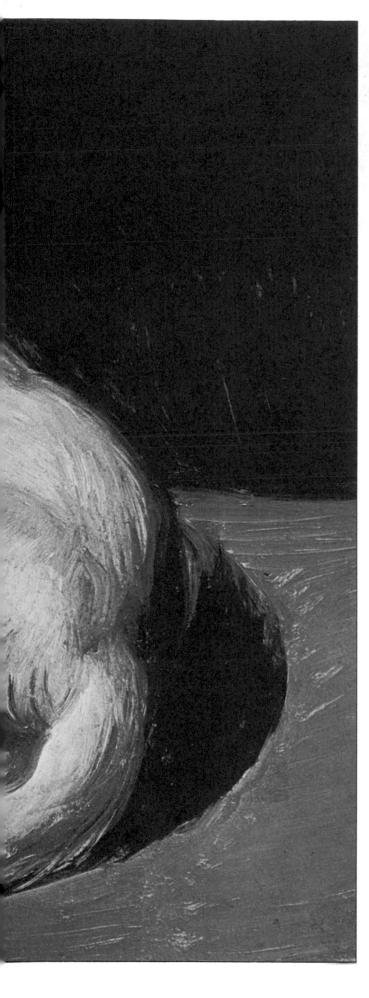

The Literary Cat

EDITED BY
Jean-Claude Suarès
and Seymour Chwast

TEXT COMPILED BY
William E. Maloney

ASSOCIATE EDITOR
Emily Blair Chewning

A Push Pin Press Book

Berkley Windhover Books

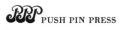 PUSH PIN PRESS

Producer: Jean-Claude Suares
Editorial Director: William E. Maloney
Design Director: Seymour Chwast

Produced by Push Pin Press
for Berkley Windhover Books

SBN: 425-03537-9 (paper)
SBN: 399-12034-3 (cloth)
Library of Congress Catalog
Card Number: 77-23583

BERKLEY WINDHOVER BOOKS
are published by Berkley Publishing
Corporation, 200 Madison Avenue,
New York, N.Y. 10016.

Printed in the United States of America.

Berkley Windhover Edition, October, 1977.

MIAO

I put down my book
The Meaning of Zen
and see the cat smiling into her fur
as she delicately combs it with her pink tongue.

"Cat, I would lend you this book to study
but it appears that you have already read it."

She looks up and gives me her full gaze.
"Don't be ridiculous," she purrs. "I wrote it."

Dilys Laing

Contents

William Butler Yeats

1865-1939

**A STROLL
WITH
EZRA POUND**

Sometimes about ten o'clock at night I accompany him to a street where there are hotels upon one side, upon the other palm-trees and the sea, and there, taking out of his pocket bones and pieces of meat, he begins to call the cats. He knows all their histories—the brindled cat looked like a skeleton until he began to feed it; that fat grey cat is an hotel proprietor's favourite, it never begs from the guests' tables and it turns cats that do not belong to the hotel out of the garden; this black cat and that grey cat over there fought on the roof of a four-storied house some weeks ago, fell off, a whirling ball of claws and fur, and now avoid each other. Yet now that I recall the scene I think that he has no affection for cats—"some of them so ungrateful", a friend says—he never nurses the café cat, I cannot imagine him with a cat of his own. Cats are oppressed, dogs terrify them, landladies starve them, boys stone them, everybody speaks of them with contempt. If they were human beings we could talk of their oppressors with a studied violence, add our strength to theirs, even organise the oppressed and like good politicians sell our charity for power. . . . *from* A Vision

**THE CAT
AND THE MOON**

The cat went here and there
And the moon spun round like a top,
And the nearest kin of the moon,
The creeping cat, looked up.
Black Minnaloushe stared at the moon,
For, wander and wail as he would,
The pure cold light in the sky
Troubled his animal blood.
Minnaloushe runs in the grass
Lifting his delicate feet.

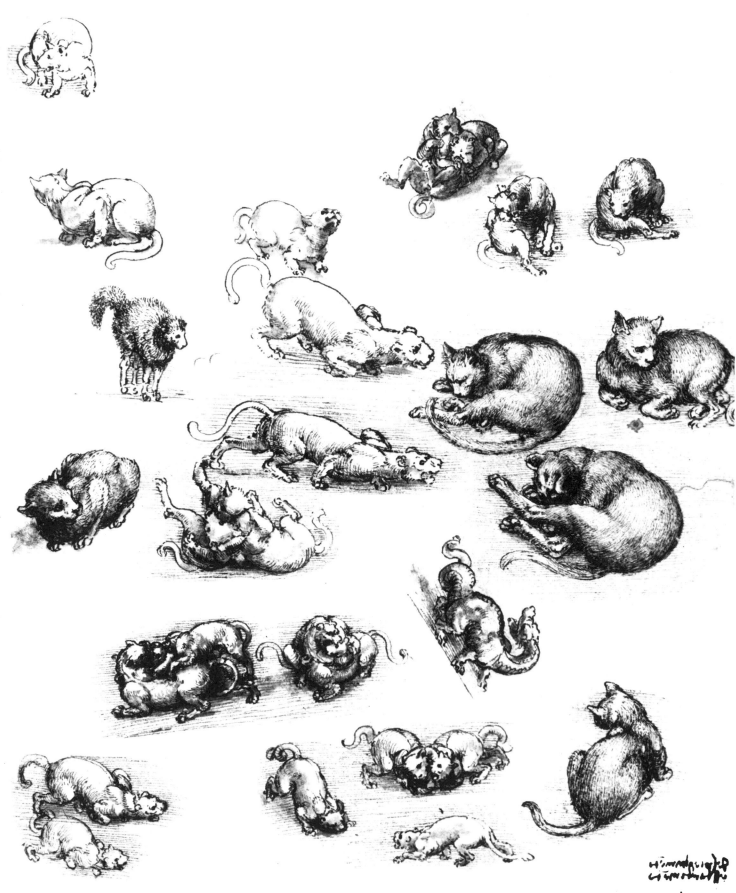

Do you dance, Minnaloushe, do you dance?
When two close kindred meet,
What better than call a dance:
Maybe the moon may learn,
Tired of that courtly fashion,
A new dance turn.
Minnaloushe creeps through the grass
From moonlit place to place,
The sacred moon overhead
Has taken a new phase.
Does Minnaloushe know that his pupils
Will pass from change to change,
And that from round to crescent,
From crescent to round they range?
Minnaloushe creeps through the grass
Alone, important and wise,
And lifts to the changing moon
His changing eyes.

Hoel, the Good

10TH CENTURY

In the time of Hoel the Good, king of Wales, who died in the year 948, laws were made as well to preserve, as to fix the different prices of animals; among which the Cat was included, as being at that period of great importance, on account of its scarcity and utility.... A General History of Quadrupeds (1791)

THE LAWS OF
HOEL THE GOOD,
PRINCE
OF SOUTH WALES

The worth of a cat and her tiethi (qualities) is this:
1. The worth of a kitten from the night it is kittened until it shall open its eyes is a legal penny.
2. And from that time, until it shall kill mice, two legal pence.
3. And after it shall kill mice, four legal pence; and so it always remains.
4. Her tiethi are, to see, to hear, to kill mice, to have her claws entire, to rear and not devour her kittens, and if she be bought, and be deficient in any one of these tiethi; let one third of her worth be returned

Of Cats:
1. The worth of a cat that is killed or stolen: its head to be put downwards upon a clean even floor, with its tail lifted upwards, and thus suspended, whilst wheat is poured about it, until the tip of its tail be covered; and that is to be its worth; if the corn cannot be had a milch sheep, with her lamb and her wool, is its value; if it be a cat which guards the King's barn.
2. The worth of a common cat is four legal pence.
3. Whoever shall sell a cat is to answer for her not going a caterwauling every moon; and that she devour not her kittens; and that she have ears, eyes, teeth and nails; and being a good mouser.

Edward Topsall

17TH CENTURY

THE HISTOIRE
OF FOUR FOOTED
BEASTES

A cat is a familiar and well knowne beast, called of the Haebrewes *Catull*, and *Schanar*, and *Schunara;* of the Graecians, *Aeluros*, and *Kattes*, and *Katis*, of the Saracens, *Katt*, the Italians *Gatta*, and *Gotto*. The Spaniards, *Katz;* the Illyrians, *Kozka;* and *Furioz* (which is used for a cat by *Albertus Magnus*), and I conjecture to be either the Persian, or the Arabian worde. The Latines call it *Feles* and sometimes *Murilegus*, and *Musio*, because it catcheth Myce, but most commonly *Catus*, which is derived of *Cautus*, signifying wary: *Ovid* faith, that when the Gyantes warred with the Goddes, the Goddes put upon them the shapes of Beasts, and the sister of *Apollo* lay for a spy in the likenes of a cat, for a cat is a watchfull and warye beast, sildome overtaken, and most attendant to her sport and prey; according to that observation of *Mantuan*:
Non fecus ae miuricatus, ille, invadere pernam
Netitur, hic rimas occulis observat acutis.
And for this cause did the Egyptians place them for hallowed Beasts, and kept them in their Temples, although they alledged the use of their skinnes for the cover of shieldes which was but an unreasonable theft, for the softnesse of a cats skinne is not fit to defend or beare a blowe.

A.C. Swinburne

1837-1909

TO A CAT

Stately, kindly, lordly friend
   Condescend
Here to sit by me, and turn
Glorious eyes that smile and burn,
Golden eyes, love's lustrous meed,
On the golden page I read.

All your wondrous wealth of hair
   Dark and fair,
Silken-shaggy, soft and bright
As the clouds and beams of night,
Pays my reverent hand's caress
Back with friendlier gentleness.

Dogs may fawn on all and some
   As they come;
You, a friend of loftier mind,
Answer friends alone in kind.
Just your foot upon my hand
Softly bids it understand.

May Swenson

1919-

THE SECRET
IN THE CAT

I took my cat apart
to see what made him purr.
Like an electric clock
or like the snore

of a warming kettle,
something fizzed and sizzled in him.
Was he a soft car,
the engine bubbling sound?

Was there a wire beneath his fur,
or humming throttle?

I undid his throat.
Within was no stir.

I opened up his chest
as though it were a door:
no whisk or rattle there.
I lifted off his skull:

no hiss or murmur.
I halved his little belly
but found no gear,
no cause for static.

So I replaced his lid,
laced his little gut.
His heart into his vest I slid
and buttoned up his throat.

His tail rose to a rod
and beckoned to the air.
Some voltage made him vibrate
warmer than before.

Whiskers and a tail:
perhaps they caught
some radar code
emitted as a pip, a dot-and-dash

of woolen sound.
My cat a kind of tuning fork?—
amplifier?—telegraph?—
doing secret signal work?

His eye elliptic tubes:
there's a message in his stare.
I stroke him
but cannot find the dial.

George Cruikshank

1792-1879

THE LADY
AS CRIES
CATS' MEAT

Old Maids your custom I invites,
    Fork out, and don't be shabby,
And don't begrudge a bit of lights
    Or liver for your Tabby.

Hark! how the Pussies make a rout—
    To buy you can't refuse;
So may you never be without
    The *music* of their *mews*.

Here's famous meat—all lean, no fat—
    No better in Great Britain;
Come, buy a penn'orth for your Cat—
    A happ'orth for your Kitten.

Come all my barrow for a bob!
    Some charity diskiver;
For faith, it ar'nt an easy job
    To *live* by selling *liver*.

Who'll buy? who'll buy of Cats-meat-Nan!
    I've bawl'd till I am sick;
But ready money is my plan;
    I never gives no tick.

I've got no customers as yet—
    In wain is my appeal—
And not to buy a single bit
    Is werry ungenteel!

Alfred Noyes

1880-1958

CATS
AND KINGS

With wide unblinking stare
    The cat looked; but she did not see the king.
She only saw a two-legg'd creature there
    Who in due time might have tit-bits to fling.

The king was on his throne.
    In his left hand he grasped the golden ball.
She looked at him with eyes of bright green stone
    And thought, *what fun if he should let it fall.*

With swishing tail she lay
    And watched for happy accidents, while he,
The essential king, was brooding far away
    In his own world of hope and memory.

O, cats are subtle now,
    And kings are mice to many a modern mind;
And yet there throbbed behind that human brow
    The strangely simple thought that serve
        mankind.

The gulf might not be wide;
    But over it, at least, no cat could spring.
So once again an ancient adage lied.
    The cat looked; but she never saw the king.

Thomas Gray
1716-1771

ODE   ON THE DEATH
OF A FAVOURITE CAT
DROWNED IN
A TUB OF
GOLD FISHES

'Twas on a lofty vase's side
    Where China's gayest art had dyed
    The azure flowers, that blow;
Demurest of the tabby kind,
The pensive Selima, reclined,
    Gazed on the lake below.

Her conscious tail her joy declared;
The fair round face, the snowy beard,
    The velvet of her paws,
Her coat, that with the tortoise vies,
Her ears of jet, and emerald eyes,
    She saw; and purr'd applause.

Still had she gazed; but 'midst the tide
Two angel forms were seen to glide,
    The genii of the stream:
Their scaly armour's Tyrian hue
Through richest purple to the view
    Betray'd a golden gleam.

The hapless nymph with wonder saw:
A whisker first, and then a claw,
    With many an ardent wish,
She stretch'd, in vain, to reach the prize
What female heart can gold despise?
    What cat's averse to fish?

Presumptuous maid! with looks intent
Again she stretch'd, again she bent,
    Nor knew the gulf between.
(Malignant Fate sat by, and smiled)

The slipp'ry verge her feet beguiled,
    She tumbled headlong in.

Eight times emerging from the flood
She mew'd to ev'ry wat'ry God,
    Some speedy aid to send.
No Dolphin came, no Nereid stirr'd:
Nor cruel Tom, nor Susan heard.
    A fav'rite has no friend!

From hence, ye beauties, undeceived,
Know, one false step is ne'er retrieved,
    And be with caution bold.
Not all that tempts your wand'ring eyes
And heedless hearts is lawful prize.
    Nor all that glitters, gold.

Mother Goose
c. 1760

PUSSY-CAT SITS
BY THE FIRE

Pussy-cat sits by the fire;
    How can she be fair?
In walks the little dog;
    Says: "Pussy, are you there?
How do you do, Mistress Pussy?
    Mistress Pussy, how d'ye do?"
"I thank you kindly, little dog,
    I fare as well as you!"

PUSSY-CAT,
PUSSY-CAT

Pussy-cat, Pussy-cat, where have you been?
I've been to London to see the Queen.
Pussy-cat, Pussy-cat, what did you there?
I frightened a little mouse under the chair.

DING-DONG-BELL

Ding-dong-bell, the cat's in the well.
    Who put her in? Little Johnny Green.
    Who pulled her out? Great Johnny Stout.
        What a naughty boy was that
        To drown a poor pussy-cat
    Who never did him any harm,
    And killed the mice in his father's barn.

MOTHER GOOSE

HEY! DIDDLE
DIDDLE.

CHARLES E. GRAHAM & CO.
NEW YORK
MADE IN U.S.A.

JINGLES

9551—Mother Goose Series

White House, 6th January 1903

Dear Kermit,

We felt very melancholy after you and Ted left and the house seemed empty and lonely. But it was the greatest possible comfort to feel that you both really have enjoyed school and are both doing well there.

Tom Quartz is certainly the cunningest kitten I have ever seen. He is always playing pranks on Jack and I get very nervous lest Jack should grow too irritated. The other evening they were both in the library—Jack sleeping before the fire—Tom Quartz scampering about, an exceedingly playful little creature—which is about what he is. He would race across the floor, then jump upon the curtain or play with the tassel. Suddenly he spied Jack and galloped up to him. Jack, looking exceedingly sullen and shame-faced, jumped out of the way and got upon the sofa and around the table, and Tom Quartz instantly jumped upon him again. Jack suddenly shifted to the other sofa, where Tom Quartz again went after him. Then Jack started for the door, while Tom made a rapid turn under the sofa and around the table and just as Jack reached the door leaped on his hind-quarters. Jack bounded forward and away and the two went tandem out of the room—Jack not co-operating at all; and about five minutes afterwards Tom Quartz stalked solemnly back.

Theodore Roosevelt

ON PUBLIC
POLICY

I cannot agree that it should be the declared public policy of Illinois that a cat visiting a neighbor's yard or crossing the highway is a public nuisance. It is the nature of cats to do a certain amount of un-escorted roaming. Many live with their owners in apartments or other restricted premises, and I doubt if we want to make their every brief foray an opportunity for a small-game hunt by zealous citizens with traps or otherwise.

I am afraid this bill could only create discord, recrimination, and enmity.

Also consider the owner's dilemma: To escort a cat abroad on a leash is against the nature of a cat, and to permit it to venture forth for exercise unat-tended into a night of new dangers is against the nature of the owner.

Moreover, cats perform useful service, partic-ularly in rural areas, in combatting rodents—work they necessarily perform alone and without regard for property lines.

We are all interested in protecting certain va-rieties of birds. That cats destroy some birds, I well know, but I believe this legislation would further but little the worthy cause to which its proponents give such unselfish effort. The problem of cat versus bird is as old as time. If we attempt to resolve it by legislation, who knows but what we may be called upon to take sides as well in the age-old problems of dog versus cat, bird versus bird, or even bird versus worm.

Adlai Stevenson

DIAMOND CUT DIAMOND

Two cats
One up a tree
One under the tree
The cat up a tree is he
The cat under the tree is she
The tree is witch elm, just incidentally.
He takes no notice of she, she takes no notice of he.
He stares at the woolly clouds passing, she stares at
The tree. There's been a lot written about cats, by
Old Possum, Yeats and Company but not Alfred de
Musset or Lord Tennyson or Poe or anybody
Wrote about one cat under, and one cat up,
A tree, Gods knows why this should be left
For me except I like cats as cats
Be especially one cat up
And one cat under
A witch elm
Tree

Ewart Milne

UNDER-THE-TABLE MANNERS

It's very hard to be polite
If you're a cat.
When other folks are up at table
Eating all that they are able,
You are down upon the mat
If you're a cat.

You're expected just to sit
If you're a cat.
Not to let them know you're there
By scratching at the chair,
Or a light, respected pat
If you're a cat.

You are not to make a fuss
If you're a cat.
Tho' there's fish upon the plate
You're expected just to wait,
Wait politely on the mat
If you're a cat.

Anonymous

18

T. S. Eliot

1888-1965

THE RUM TUM TUGGER

The Rum Tum Tugger is a Curious Cat:
If you offer him pheasant he would rather have
    grouse.
If you put him in a house he would much prefer
    a flat,
If you put him in a flat then he'd rather have a
    house.
If you set him on a mouse then he only wants a rat,
If you set him on a rat then he'd rather chase a
    mouse.
Yes the Rum Tum Tugger is a Curious Cat—
    And there isn't any call for me to shout it:
      For he will do
      As he do do
        And there's no doing anything about it!

The Rum Tum Tugger is a terrible bore:
When you let him in, then he wants to be out;
He's always on the wrong side of every door,
And as soon as he's at home, then he'd like to get
    about.
He likes to lie in the bureau drawer,
But he makes such a fuss if he can't get out.
Yes the Rum Tum Tugger is a Curious Cat—
    And it isn't any use for you to doubt it:
      For he will do
      As he do do
        And there's no doing anything about it!

The Rum Tum Tugger is a curious beast:
His disobliging ways are a matter of habit.
If you offer him fish then he always wants a feast;
When there isn't any fish then he won't eat rabbit.
If you offer him cream then he sniffs and sneers,
For he only likes what he finds for himself;
So you'll catch him in it right up to the ears,
If you put it away on the larder shelf.
The Rum Tum Tugger is artful and knowing,
The Rum Tum Tugger doesn't care for a cuddle;
But he'll leap on your lap in the middle of your
    sewing,
For there's nothing he enjoys like a horrible
    muddle.
Yes the Rum Tum Tugger is a Curious Cat—

And there isn't any need for me to spout it:
    For he will do
    As he do do
      And there's no doing anything about it!

THE NAMING OF CATS

The Naming of Cats is a difficult matter,
    It isn't just one of your holiday games;
You may think at first I'm as mad as a hatter
When I tell you, a cat must have THREE DIFFERENT
    NAMES.
First of all, there's the name that the family use
    daily,
    Such as Peter, Augustus, Alonzo or James,
Such as Victor or Jonathan, George or Bill
    Bailey—
    All of them sensible everyday names.
There are fancier names if you think they sound
    sweeter,
    Some for the gentlemen, some for the dames:
Such as Plato, Admetus, Electra, Demeter—
    But all of them sensible everyday names.
But I tell you, a cat needs a name that's particular,
    A name that's peculiar, and more dignified,
Else how can he keep up his tail perpendicular,
    Or spread out his whiskers, or cherish his pride?
Of names of this kind, I can give you a quorum.
    Such as Munkustrap, Quaxo, or Coricopat,
Such as Bombalurina, or else Jellylorum—
    Names that never belong to more than one cat.
But above and beyond there's still one name left
    over,
    And that is the name that you never will guess;
The name that no human research can discover—
    But THE CAT HIMSELF KNOWS, and will never
      confess.
When you notice a cat in profound meditation,
    The reason, I tell you, is always the same:
His mind is engaged in a rapt contemplation
    Of the thought, of the thought, of the thought of
      his name:
      His ineffable effable
      Effanineffable
Deep and inscrutable singular Name.

THE SONG OF THE JELLICLES

Jellicle Cats come out to-night
Jellicle Cats come one come all:
The Jellicle Moon is shining bright—
Jellicles come to the Jellicle Ball.

Jellicle Cats are black and white,
Jellicle Cats are rather small;
Jellicle Cats are merry and bright,
And pleasant to hear when they caterwaul.
Jellicle Cats have cheerful faces,
Jellicle Cats have bright black eyes;
They like to practise their airs and graces
And wait for the Jellicle Moon to rise.

Jellicle Cats develop slowly,
Jellicle Cats are not too big;
Jellicle Cats are roly-poly,
They know how to dance a gavotte and a jig.
Until the Jellicle Moon appears
They make their toilette and take their repose:
Jellicles wash behind their ears,
Jellicles dry between their toes.

Jellicle Cats are white and black,
Jellicle Cats are of moderate size;
Jellicles jump like a jumping-jack,
Jellicle Cats have moonlit eyes.

They're quiet enough in the morning hours,
They're quiet enough in the afternoon,
Reserving their terpsichorean powers
To dance by the light of the Jellicle Moon.

Jellicle Cats are black and white,
Jellicle Cats (as I said) are small;
If it happens to be a stormy night
They will practise a caper or two in the hall.
If it happens the sun is shining bright
You would say they had nothing to do at all:
They are resting and saving themselves to be right
For the Jellicle Moon and the Jellicle Ball.

THREE TABBIES

Three tabbies took out their cats to tea,
As well-behaved tabbies as well could be:
Each sat in the chair that each preferred,
They mewed for their milk, and they sipped and
    purred.
Now tell me this (as these cats you've seen them)—
How many lives had these cats between them?

Kate Greenaway

Very much do I love cats, and I suppose that I could
write a large book about the different cats that I
have kept in various climes and times, on both sides
of the world.

Lafcadio Hearn

20

The Cat

As Cousin Kate and Tiptoes and Nannie and Fred sat looking at the "pussy-cat picture," as Tiptoes called it, Uncle Willie came in, bringing Nannie's gray kitty. Uncle Willie wore his flowered dressing-gown, his tasselled cap, and a long red scarf around his waist.

"Ladies and gentlemen," said he, "I am a brave and valiant showman, and I have come to show you one of the most remarkable and interesting animals in the world. Its English name is *Cat*, but in China it is called the '*Miao*.' To begin with, the cat is a beautiful animal. Look, gentlemen and ladies, at her richly shaded and silky fur; her slender limbs; her tail, tapering smoothly to a point! How easily she bends her body! How lightly she springs! And how lightly she falls!" added Uncle Willie, as kitty sprang down to chase a rolling cotton-spool. "If Tiptoes were lying on the floor, playing with a spool, he could not move his neck and legs and arms in that graceful way.

"In the next place, the cat is a wonderful animal. Kitty jumped from a place five times her own height. If Tiptoes were to jump from a place five times his own height,—the chamber window, for instance,—he would probably break his bones. But the cat is light for her size, and the cat is flexible, that is, her body bends easily. It bends easily because the skin is placed loosely upon it, and because the joints of the backbone are so formed that this backbone can be curved in any direction. Another reason why the cat falls lightly is that her feet are elastic. India-rubber is elastic, you know. An india-rubber ball does not fall with a thump, it touches and bounds back. If the bottoms of our feet were provided with thick cushions made of india-rubber and velvet, and if we were sure of coming down upon our toes, we might dare to jump from a high window, especially if we had four such feet. The cat, having elastic cushions on her feet, and four such feet, and the faculty of alighting upon her toes, and a loose skin, and a light, flexible body, is wonderfully contrived for jumping from high places.

from Prang's Natural History Series
For Children, 19th Century.

COMMON CAT.

Cat Family

Lith and Publ. by L. Prang & Co.

THE DOMESTIC CAT

The manners and disposition of the Cat seems to be entirely changed by education; and, although it does not exhibit towards mankind the affection of the Dog, yet it is by no means destitute either of gentleness or gratitude. These animals are not, like the Dog, attached to our persons: their chief attachment seems to be to the houses in which they have been brought up. Instances are not uncommon of Cats having returned, of their own accord, to the place from which they have been carried; though at the distance of many miles, and even across rivers where they could not possibly have had any knowledge either of the road, or of the direction that would lead them to it. This local attachment may perhaps arise from their having been acquainted, in their former habitations, with all the retreats of the Mice, and the passages and outlets of the house; and from the disadvantages which they must experience in these particulars by changing their residence.

Few animals exhibit more maternal tenderness, or show a greater love for their offspring, than the Cat. The assiduity with which she attends them, and the pleasure which she seems to take in all their playful tricks, afford a grateful entertainment to every observer of nature. She has also been known not only to nurse with tenderness the offspring of different individuals of her own species, but even those of other kinds of animals.

A friends of the Rev. Mr. White of Selborne, had a little helpless *Leveret* brought to him, which the servants fed with milk from a spoon; and about the same time his Cat kittened, and her young-ones were destroyed. The Hare was soon lost; and was supposed to have been killed by some Dog or Cat. About a fortnight afterwards, as its owner was sitting in his garden, in the dusk of the evening, he observed his Cat, with tail erect, trotting towards him, and calling with little short inward notes of complacency, (such as these animals use towards their Kittens,) to something gambolling after her, which proved to be the Leveret, that the Cat had nourished with her milk, and continued to support with great affection. Thus was a grameniverous animal nurtured by a carnivorous and predacious one! This strange affection in the Cat was probably occasioned by those tender maternal feelings, which the loss of her Kittens had awakened; and by the complacency and ease she had derived from having her teats drawn, when too much distended with milk. From habit, she became as much delighted with this foundling, as if it had been her real offspring.

A boy (Mr. White says) brought to him three young Squirrels which had been taken from their nest. These little creatures he put under a Cat that had recently lost her Kittens; and he found that she nursed and suckled them with the same assiduity and affection as if they had been her own progeny. So many persons, however, went to see the little Squirrels suckled by a Cat, that the foster-mother became jealous of her charge, and in pain for their safety; and therefore hid them over the ceiling, where one of them died.

Some years ago a sympathy of this nature took place, in the house of Mr. James Greenfield, of Maryland, between a *Cat and a Rat*. The Cat had Kittens, to which she frequently carried Mice, and other small animals for food; and among the rest

she is supposed to have carried them a young Rat. The Kittens, probably not being hungry, played with it: and when the Cat gave suck to them, the Rat likewise sucked her. This having been observed by some of the servants, Mr. Greenfield was informed of it. He had the Kittens and Rat brought down stairs and put on the floor; and in carrying them off, the Cat was remarked to convey away the young Rat as tenderly as she did any of the Kittens. This experiment was repeated as often as any company came to the house, till a great number of persons had become eye witnesses of the extraordinary affection.

Cats, by means of their whiskers, seem to possess something like an additional sense; these have, perhaps, some analogy to the antennae of moths and butterflies. They consist not only of long hairs on the upper lip, but also of four or five long hairs standing up from each eye-brow, and two or three on each cheek; all which, when the animal erects them, make, with their extremities, so many points in the periphery of a circle, equal, at least, in extent, to the circumference of their own bodies. With this instrument, it is supposed that, by a little experience, they can at once discover whether any aperture among hedges or shrubs (in which animals of this genus live in their wild state) is large enough to admit their bodies; to them a matter of the greatest consequence, whether pursuing or pursued. They have likewise the power of erecting and bringing forward the whiskers on their lips, which probably is for the purpose of feeling whether a dark hole be permeable or not.

It is generally supposed that Cats are able to see in the dark; but, although this is not absolutely the case, it is certain that they can see with much less light than most other animals; owing to the peculiar structure of their eyes, the pupils of which are capable of being contracted or dilated in proportion to the degree of light by which they are affected. In the day-time, the pupil of the Cat's eye is perpetually contracted, and sometimes into a mere line; for it is with difficulty that this animal can see by a strong light: but in the twilight the pupil resumes its natural roundness, and the animal enjoys perfect vision.

In order to preserve their fur clean, Cats wash their faces, and generally quite behind their ears, every time they eat. As they can not lick those places with their tongues, they first wet the inside of their leg with the saliva, and then repeatedly rub them over with it. This Dr. Darwin, whimsically enough, esteems an act of reasoning; "because," he says, "a means is used to produce an effect; which means seem to be acquired by imitation, like the greater part of human arts."

The fur of the Cat, being generally clean and dry, readily yields electric sparks when rubbed; and, if a clean and perfectly dry Domestic Cat be placed, in frosty weather, on a stool with glass feet, or be insulated by any other means, and rubbed for a little time in contact with the wire of a coated vial, the vial will become charged.

No experiment can be more beautiful than that of sitting a Kitten, for the first time, before a looking-glass. The animal appears surprised and pleased with the resemblance, and makes several attempts to touch its new acquaintance; and, at length, finding its efforts fruitless, it looks behind the glass, and appears astonished at the absence of the figure. It again views itself, and tries to touch the image with its foot, suddenly looking at intervals behind the glass. It then becomes more accurate in its observations; and begins, as it were, to make experiments, by stretching out its paw in different directions; and when it finds that these motions are answered in every respect by the figure in the glass, it seems, at length, to be convinced of the real nature of the image.

The following curious fact in the natural history of the Cat, is related by Dr. Anderson, in his Recreations in Agriculture: a Cat belonging to Dr. Coventry, the ingenious Professor of Agriculture in Edinburg, had no blemish at its birth, but lost its tail by accident when it was young. This Cat had many litters of Kittens; and in every litter there was one or more that wanted the tail, either wholly or in part.

"A Cat," says Browne, in his Natural History of Jamaica, "is a very dainty dish among the Negroes."

from The History of Animals, *19th Century*

Théophile Gautier

1811-1872

THE WHITE
AND BLACK
DYNASTIES

A cat brought from Havana by Mademoiselle Aïta de la Penuela, a young Spanish artist whose studies of white angoras may still be seen gracing the printsellers' windows, produced the daintiest little kitten imaginable. It was just like a swan's-down powder-puff, and on account of its immaculate whiteness it received the name of Pierrot. When it grew big this was lengthened to Don Pierrot de Navarre as being more grandiose and majestic.

Don Pierrot, like all animals which are spoiled and made much of, developed a charming amiability of character. He shared the life of the household with all the pleasure which cats find in the intimacy of the domestic hearth. Seated in his usual place near the fire, he really appeared to understand what was being said, and to take an interest in it. His eyes followed the speakers, and from time to time he would utter little sounds, as though he too wanted to make remarks and give his opinion on literature, which was our usual topic of conversation. He was very fond of books, and when he found one open on a table he would lie on it, look at the page attentively, and turn over the leaves with his paw; then he would end by going to sleep, for all the world as if he were reading a fashionable novel.

Directly I took up a pen he would jump on my writing-desk and with deep attention watch the steel nib tracing black spider-legs on the expanse of white paper, and his head would turn each time I began a new line. Sometimes he tried to take part in the work, and would attempt to pull the pen out of my hand, no doubt in order to write himself, for he was an aesthetic cat, like Hoffman's Murr, and I strongly suspect him of having scribbled his memoirs at night on some house-top by the light of his phosphorescent eyes. Unfortunately these lucubrations have been lost.

Don Pierrot never went to bed until I came in. He waited for me inside the door, and as I entered the hall he would rub himself against my legs and arch his back, purring joyfully all the time. Then he proceeded to walk in front of me like a page, and if I had asked him, he would certainly have carried the candle for me. In this fashion he escorted me to my room and waited while I undressed; then he would jump on the bed, put his paws round my neck, rub noses with me, and lick me with his rasping little pink tongue, while giving vent to soft inarticulate cries, which clearly expressed how pleased he was to see me again. Then when his transports of affection had subsided, and the hour for repose had come, he would balance himself on the rail of the bedstead and sleep there like a bird perched on a bough. When I woke in the morning he would come and lie near me until it was time to get up. Twelve o'clock was the hour at which I was supposed to come in. On this subject Pierrot had all the notions of a concierge.

At that time we had instituted little evening gatherings among a few friends, and had formed a small society, which we called the Four Candles Club, the room in which we met being, as it happened, lit by four candles in silver candlesticks, which were placed at the corners of the table.

Sometimes the conversation became so lively that I forgot the time, at the risk of finding, like Cinderella, my carriage turned into a pumpkin and my coachman into a rat.

Pierrot waited for me several times until two o'clock in the morning, but in the end my conduct displeased him, and he went to bed without me. This mute protest against my innocent dissipation touched me so much that ever after I came home regularly at midnight. But it was a long time before Pierrot forgave me. He wanted to be sure that it was not a sham repentance; but when he was convinced of the sincerity of my conversion, he deigned to take me into favour again, and he resumed his nightly post in the entrance-hall.

To gain the friendship of a cat is not an easy thing. It is a philosophic, well-regulated, tranquil animal, a creature of habit and a lover of order and cleanliness. It does not give its affections indiscriminately. It will consent to be your friend if you are worthy of the honour, but it will not be your slave. With all its affection, it preserves its freedom of judgment, and it will not do anything for you which it considers unreasonable; but once it has given its love, what absolute confidence, what fidelity of affection! It will make itself the companion of your hours of work, of loneliness, or of sadness. It will lie the whole evening on your knee, purring and happy in your society, and leaving the company of creatures of its own kind to be with you. In vain the sound of caterwauling reverberates from the house-tops, inviting it to one of those cats' evening parties where essence of hed-herring takes the place of tea. It will not be tempted, but continues to keep its vigil with you. If you put it down it climbs up again quickly, with a sort of crooning noise, which is like a gentle reproach. Sometimes, when seated in front of you, it gazes at you with such soft, melting eyes, such a human and caressing look, that you are almost awed, for it seems impossible that reason can be absent from it.

Don Pierrot had a companion of the same race as himself, and no less white. All the imaginable snowy comparisons it were possible to pile up would not suffice to give an idea of that immaculate fur, which would have made ermine look yellow.

I called her Seraphita, in memory of Balzac's Swedenborgian romance. The heroine of that wonderful story, when she climbed the snow peaks of the Falberg with Minna, never shone with a more pure white radiance. Seraphita had a dreamy and pensive character. She would lie motionless on a cushion for hours, not asleep, but with eyes fixed in rapt attention on scenes invisible to ordinary mortals.

Caresses were agreeable to her, but she responded to them with great reserve, and only to those of people whom she favoured with her esteem, which it was not easy to gain. She liked luxury, and it was always in the newest armchair or on the piece of furniture best calculated to show off her swan

like beauty, that she was to be found. Her toilette took an immense time. She would carefully smooth her entire coat every morning, and wash her face with her paw, and every hair on her body shone like new silver when brushed by her pink tongue. If anyone touched her she would immediately efface all traces of the contact, for she could not endure being ruffled. He elegance and distinction gave one an idea of aristocratic birth, and among her own kind she must have been at least a duchess. She had a passion for scents. She would plunge her nose into bouquets, and nibble a perfumed handkerchief with little paroxysms of delight. She would walk about on the dressing-table sniffing the stoppers of the scent-bottles, and she would have loved to use the violet powder if she had been allowed.

Such was Seraphita, and never was a cat more worthy of a poetic name.

Don Pierrot de Navarre, being a native of Havana, needed a hot-house temperature. This he found indoors, but the house was surrounded by large gardens, divided up by palings through which a cat could easily slip, and planted with big trees in which hosts of birds twittered and sang; and sometimes Pierrot, taking advantage of an open door, would go out hunting of an evening and run over the dewy grass and flowers. He would then have to wait till morning to be let in again, for although he might come mewing under the windows, his appeal did not always wake the sleepers inside.

He had a delicate chest, and one colder night than usual he took a chill which soon developed into consumption. Poor Pierrot, after a year of coughing, became wasted and thin, and his coat, which formerly boasted such a snowy gloss, now put one in mind of the lustreless white of a shroud. His great limpid eyes looked enormous in his attenuated face. His pink nose had grown pale, and he would walk sadly along the sunny wall with slow steps, and watch the yellow autumn leaves whirling up in spirals. He looked as though he were reciting Millevoye's elegy.

There is nothing more touching than a sick animal; it submits to suffering with such gentle, pathetic resignation.

Everything possible was done to try and save Pierrot. He had a very clever doctor who sounded him and felt his pulse. He ordered him asses' milk, which the poor creature drank willingly enough out of his little china saucer. He lay for hours on my knee like the ghost of a sphinx, and I could feel the bones of his spine like the beads of a rosary under my fingers. He tried to respond to my caresses with

THE NIGHT CREATURES

A Cat, with its phosphorescent eyes that shine like lanterns, and sparks flashing from its back, moves fearlessly through the darkness, where it meets wandering ghosts, witches, alchemists, necromancers, grave-robbers, lovers, thieves, murderers, grey-cloaked patrols, and all the obscene larvae that only emerge at night.

Theophile Gautier

a feeble purr which was like a death rattle.

When he was dying he lay panting on his side, but with a supreme effort he raised himself and came to me with dilated eyes in which there was a look of intense supplication. This look seemed to say: "Cannot you save me, you who are a man?" Then he staggered a short way with eyes already glazing, and fell down with such a lamentable cry, so full of despair and anguish, that I was pierced with silent horror.

He was buried at the bottom of the garden under a white rosebush which still marks his grave.

Seraphita died two or three years later of diphtheria, against which no science could prevail.

She rests not far from Pierrot. With her the white dynasty became extinct, but not the family. To this snow-white pair were born three kittens as black as ink.

Let him explain this mystery who can.

Just at that time Victor Hugo's *Misérables* was in great vogue, and the names of the characters in the novel were on everyone's lips. I called the two male kittens Enjolras and Gavroche, while the little female received the name of Eponine.

They were perfectly charming in their youth. I trained them like dogs to fetch and carry a bit of paper crumpled into a ball, which I threw for them. In time they learnt to fetch it from the tops of cupboards, from behind chests or from the bottom of tall vases, out of which they would pull it very cleverly with their paws. When they grew up they disdained such frivolous games, and acquired that calm philosophic temperament which is the true nature of cats.

To people landing in America in a slave colony all negroes are negroes, and indistinguishable from one another. In the same way, to careless eyes, three black cats are three black cats; but attentive observers make no such mistake. Animal physiognomy varies as much as that of men, and I could distinguish perfectly between those faces, all three as black as Harlequin's mask, and illuminated by emerald disks shot with gold.

Enjolras was by far the handsomest of the three. He was remarkable for his great leonine head and big ruff, his powerful shoulders, long back and splendid feathery tail. There was something theatrical about him, and he seemed to be always posing like a popular actor who knows he is being admired. His movements were slow, undulating and majestic. He put each foot down with as much circumspection as if he were walking on a table covered with Chinese bric-à-brac or Venetian glass. As to his character, he was by no means a stoic, and he showed a love of eating which that virtuous and sober young man, his namesake, would certainly have disapproved. Enjolras would undoubtedly have said to him, like the angel to Swedenborg: "You eat too much."

I humoured this gluttony, which was as amusing as a gastronomic monkey's, and Enjolras attained a size and weight seldom reached by the domestic cat. It occurred to me to have him shaved poodle-fashion, so as to give the finishing touch to his resemblance to a lion.

We left him his mane and a big tuft at the end of his tail, and I would not swear that we did not give him mutton-chop whiskers on his haunches like those Munito wore. Thus thricked out, it must be confessed he was much more like a Japanese monster than an African lion. Never was a more fantastic whim carved out of a living animal. His shaven skin took odd blue tints, which contrasted strangely with his black mane.

Gavroche, as though desirous of calling to mind his namesake in the novel, was a cat with an arch and crafty expression of countenance. He was smaller than Enjolras, and his movements were comically quick and brusque. In him absurd capers and ludicrous postures took the place of the banter and slang of the Parisian gamin. It must be confessed that Gavroche had vulgar tastes. He seized every possible occasion to leave the drawing-room in order to go and make up parties in the back-yard, or even in the street, with stray cats, "De naissance quelconque et de sang peu prouvé," in which doubtful company he completely forgot his dignity as cat of Havana, son of Don Pierrot de Navarre, grandee of Spain of the first order, and of the aristocratic and haughty Doña Seraphita.

Sometimes in his truant wanderings he picked up emaciated comrades, lean with hunger, and brought them to his plate of food to give them a treat in his good-natured, lordly way. The poor creatures, with ears laid back and watchful side-glances, in fear of being interrupted in their free meal by the broom of the housemaid, swallowed double, triple, and quadruple mouthfuls, and, like the famous dog Siete-Aguas (seven waters) of Spanish *posadas* (inns), they licked the plate as clean as if it had been washed and polished by one of Gerard Dow's or Mieris's Dutch housewives.

Seeing Gavroche's friends reminded me of a phrase which illustrates one of Gavarni's drawings, "Ils sont jolis les amis dont vous etes susceptible d'aller avec!" ("Pretty kind of friends you like to associate with!")

But that only proved what a good heart Gavroche

had, for he could easily have eaten all the food himself.

The cat named after the interesting Eponine was more delicate and slender than her brothers. Her nose was rather long, and her eyes slightly oblique, and green as those of Pallas Athene, to whom Homer always applied the epithet of γλαυκῶπις. Her nose was of velvety black, with the grain of a fine Périgord truffle; her whiskers were in a perpetual state of agitation, all of which gave her a peculiarly expressive countenance. Her superb black coat was always in motion, and was watered and shot with shadowy markings. Never was there a more sensitive, nervous, electric animal. If one stroked her two or three times in the dark, blue sparks would fly crackling out of her fur.

Eponine attached herself particularly to me, like the Eponine of the novel to Marius, but I, being less taken up with Cosette than that handsome young man, could accept the affection of this gentle and devoted cat, who still shares the pleasures of my suburban retreat, and is the inseparable companion of my hours of work.

She comes running up when she hears the front-door bell, receives the visitors, conducts them to the drawing-room, talks to them—yes, talks to them —with little chirruping sounds, that do not in the least resemble the language cats use in talking to their own kind, but which simulate the articulate speech of man. What does she say? She says in the clearest way, "Will you be good enough to wait till monsieur comes down? Please look at the pictures, or chat with me in the meantime, if that will amuse you." Then when I come in she discreetly retires to an armchair or a corner of the piano, like a well-bred animal who knows what is correct in good society. Pretty little Eponine gave so many proofs of intelligence, good disposition and sociability, that by common consent she was raised to the dignity of a *person*, for it was quite evident that she was possessed of higher reasoning power than mere instinct. This dignity conferred on her the privilege of eating at table like a person instead of out of a saucer in a corner of the room like an animal.

So Eponine had a chair next to me at breakfast and dinner, but on account of her small size she was allowed to rest her two front paws on the edge of the table. Her place was laid, without spoon or fork, but she had her glass. She went right through dinner dish by dish, from soup to dessert, waiting for her turn to be helped, and behaving with such propriety and nice manners as one would like to see in many children. She made her appearance at the first sound of the bell, and on going into the dining-room one found her already in her place, sitting up in her chair with her paws resting on the edge of the table-cloth, and seeming to offer you her little face to kiss, like a well-brought-up little girl who is affectionately polite towards her parents and elders.

As one finds flaws in diamonds, spots on the sun, and shadows on perfection itself, so Eponine, it must be confessed, had a passion for fish. She shared this in common with all other cats. Contrary to the Latin proverb, "Catus amat pisces, sed non vult tingere plantas," she would willingly have dipped her paw into the water if by so doing she could have pulled out a trout or a young carp. She became nearly frantic over fish, and, like a child who is filled with the expectation of dessert, she sometimes rebelled at her soup when she knew (from previous investigations in the kitchen) that fish was coming. When this happened she was not helped, and I would say to her coldly: "Mademoiselle, a person who is not hungry for soup cannot be hungry for fish," and the dish would be pitilessly carried away from under her nose. Convinced that matters were serious, greedy Eponine would swallow her soup in all haste, down to the last drop, polishing off the last crumb of bread or bit of macaroni, and would them turn round and look at me with pride, like someone who has conscientiously done his duty. She was then given her portion, which she consumed with great satisfaction, and after tasting of every dish in turn, she would finish up by drinking a third of a glass of water.

When I am expecting friends to dinner Eponine knows there is going to be a party before she sees the guests. She looks at her place, and if she sees a knife and fork by her plate she decamps at once and seats herself on a music-stool, which is her refuge on these occasions.

Let those who deny reasoning powers to animals explain if they can this little fact, apparently so simple, but which contains a whole series of inductions. From the presence near her plate of those implements which man alone can use, this observant and reflective cat concludes that she will have to give up her place for that day to a guest, and promptly proceeds to do so. She never makes a mistake; but when she knows the visitor well she climbs on his knee and tries to coax a tit-bit out of him by her pretty caressing ways.

When I play with my cat, who knows whether she diverts herself with me, or I with her. *Montaigne*

Henry David Thoreau

1817-1862

MIN MISSES
A MOUSE

Min caught a mouse, and was playing with it in the yard. It had got away from her once or twice and she had caught it again, and now it was stealing off again, as she was complacently watching it with her paws tucked under her, when her friend, Riorden, a stout cock, stepped up inquisitively, looked down at the mouse with one eye, turning its head, then picked it up by the tail, gave it two or three whacks on the ground, and giving it a dexterous toss in the air, caught the mouse in its open mouth. It went, head foremost and alive, down Riorden's capacious throat in the twinkling of an eye, never again to be seen in this world; Min all the while, with paws comfortably tucked under her, looking on unconcerned. What did one mouse matter, more or less, to her? The cock walked off amid the currant-bushes, stretched his neck up and gulped once or twice, and the deed was accomplished. Then he crowed lustily in celebration of the exploit. It might be set down among the *Gesta gallorum*. There were several human witnesses. It is a question whether Min ever understood where that mouse went to. She sits composedly sentinel, with paws tucked under her, a good part of her days at present, by some ridiculous little hole, the possible entry of a mouse.

Aesop

c. 6TH CENTURY B.C.

THE CAT
AND THE MICE

A cat, grown feeble with age, and no longer able to hunt for mice as she was wont to do, sat in the sun and bethought herself how she might entice them within reach of her paws.

The idea came to her that if she would suspend herself by the hind legs from a peg in the closet wall, the mice, believing her to be dead, no longer would be afraid of her. So, at great pains and with the assistance of a torn pillow case she was able to

carry out her plan.

But before the mice could approach within range of the innocent-looking paws a wise old gaffer-mouse whispered to his friends: "Keep your distance, my friends. Many a bag have I seen in my day, but never one with a cat's head at the bottom of it."

Then turning to the uncomfortable feline, he said: "Hang there, good madam, as long as you please, but I would not trust myself within reach of you though you were stuffed with straw."

Application: HE WHO IS ONCE DECEIVED IS DOUBLY CAUTIOUS.

John Keats
1795-1821

TO A CAT

Cat! who has pass'd thy grand climacteric,
How many mice and rats hast in thy days
Destroy'd?—How many titbits stolen? Gaze
With those bright languid segments green, and prick
Those velvet ears—but prithee do not stick
Thy latent talons in me—and upraise
Thy gentle mew—and tell me all thy frays
Of fish and mice, and rats and tender chick.

Nay, look not down, nor lick thy dainty wrists—
For all the wheezy asthma—and for all
Thy tail's tip is nick'd off—and though the fists
Of many a maid have given thee many a maul,
Still is that fur as soft as when the lists
In youth thou enter'dst on glass-bottled wall.

Lewis Carroll
1832-1898

ALICE IN
WONDERLAND

But I don't want to go among mad people," Alice remarked.

"Oh, you ca'n't help that," said the Cat: "we're all mad here. I'm mad. You're mad."

"How do you know I'm mad?" said Alice.

"You must be," said the Cat, "or you wouldn't come here."

THE MOUSE'S
TALE

We lived beneath the mat,
      Warm and snug and fat,
            But one woe, and that
                  Was the Cat!

————

                  To our joys
                  a clog, In
                  our eyes a
                  fog, On our
                  hearts a log,
                  Was the Dog!

————

            When the
      Cat's away,
   Then
The mice
   will
      play,
         But alas!
            one day, (So they say)

————

                  Came the Dog and
                  Cat, hunting
                        for a
                  Rat,
                  Crushed
                  the mice
               all flat,
            Each
         one
          as
           he
            sat,
             Underneath the mat, Warm and safe and fat. Think of that!

I had only one cat, and he was more a companion than a cat. When he departed this life I did not care to, as many men do when their partners die, take a second.

Charles Dudley Warner

James Thurber
1894-1961

Ⓞne thing was certain, that the *white* kitten had had nothing to do with it:—it was the black kitten's fault entirely. For the white kitten had been having its face washed by the old cat for the last quarter of an hour (and bearing it pretty well, considering); so you see that it *couldn't* have had any hand in the mischief.

The way Dinah washed her children's faces was this: first she held the poor thing down by its ear with one paw, and then with the other paw she rubbed its face all over, the wrong way, beginning at the nose: and just now, as I said, she was hard at work on the white kitten, which was lying quite still and trying to purr—no doubt feeling that it was all meant for its good.

But the black kitten had been finished with earlier in the afternoon, and so, while Alice was sitting curled up in a corner of the great arm-chair, half talking to herself and half asleep, the kitten had been having a grand game of romps with the ball of worsted Alice had been trying to wind up, and had been rolling it up and down till it had all come undone again; and there it was, spread over the hearth-rug, all knots and tangles, with the kitten running after its own tail in the middle.

'Oh, you wicked wicked little thing!' cried Alice, catching up the kitten, and giving it a little kiss to make it understand that it was in disgrace. 'Really, Dinah ought to have taught you better manners! You *ought*, Dinah, you know you ought!' she added, looking reproachfully at the old cat, and speaking in as cross a voice as she could manage— and then she scrambled back into the arm-chair, taking the kitten and the worsted with her, and began winding up the ball again. But she didn't get on very fast, as she was talking all the time, sometimes to the kitten, and sometimes to herself. Kitty sat very demurely on her knee, pretending to watch the progress of the winding, and now and then putting out one paw and gently touching the ball, as if it would be glad to help if it might.

L.C.

A dog is okay
On a sunny day
But a cat
Is where it's at.

Paula Scher

Q. Our cat, who is thirty-five, spends all of her time in bed. She follows every move I make, and this is beginning to get to me. She never seems sleepy nor particularly happy. Is there anything I could give her?   MISS L. MC.

A. There are no medicines which can safely be given to induce felicity in a cat, but you might try lettuce, which is a soporific, for the wakefulness. I would have to see the cat watching you to tell whether anything could be done to divert her attention.

Q. We have cats the way most people have mice.   MRS. C. L. FOOTLOOSE

A. I see you have. I can't tell from your communication, however, whether you wish advice or are just boasting.

Edward Lear
1817-1888

The Seven young Cats set off on their travels with great delight and rapacity. But, on coming to the top of a high hill, they perceived at a long distance off a Clangle-Wangle (or, as it is more properly written, Clangel-Wangel), and in spite of the warning they had had, they ran straight up to it.

(Now the Clangle-Wangle is a most dangerous and delusive beast, and by no means commonly to be met with. They live in the water as well as on land, using their long tail as a sail when in the former element. Their speed is extreme, but their habits of life are domestic and superfluous, and their general demeanour pensive and pellucid. On summer evenings they may sometimes be observed near the Lake Pipple-popple, standing on their heads and humming their national melodies: they subsist entirely on vegetables, excepting when they eat veal, or mutton, or pork, or beef, or fish, or saltpetre.)

The moment the Clangle-Wangle saw the Seven young Cats approach, he ran away; and as he ran straight on for four months, and the Cats, though they continued to run, could never overtake him,— they all gradually *died* of fatigue and of exhaustion, and never afterwards recovered.

And this was the end of the Seven young Cats.

C was Papa's gray Cat,
    What caught a squeaky Mouse;
She pulled him by his twirly tail
    All about the house.

THE OWL
AND THE
PUSSY-CAT

I

The Owl and the Pussy-cat went to sea
    In a beautiful pea-green boat,
They took some honey, and plenty of money,
    Wrapped up in a five-pound note.
The Owl looked up to the stars above,
    And sang to a small guitar,
'O lovely Pussy! O Pussy, my love,
        What a beautiful Pussy you are,
            You are,
            You are!
    What a beautiful Pussy you are!'
And hand in hand, on the edge of the sand,
    They danced by the light of the moon,
        The moon,
        The moon,
They danced by the light of the moon.

II

Pussy said to the Owl, 'You elegant fowl!
    How charmingly sweet you sing!
O let us be married! too long we have tarried:
    But what shall we do for a ring?'
They sailed away, for a year and a day,
    To the land where the Bong-tree grows
And there in a wood a Piggy-wig stood
    With a ring at the end of his nose,
        His nose,
        His nose,
With a ring at the end of his nose.

III

'Dear Pig, are you willing to sell for one shilling
    Your ring?' Said the Piggy, 'I will.'
So they took it away, and were married next day
    By the Turkey who lives on the hill.
They dined on mince, and slices of quince,
    Which they ate with a runcible spoon;
And hand in hand, on the edge of the sand,
    They danced by the light of the moon,
        The moon,
        The moon,
They danced by the light of the moon.

Ogden Nash
1902-1971

THE KITTEN

The trouble with a kitten is
THAT
Eventually it becomes a
CAT.

THE CAT

You get a wife, you get a house,
Eventually you get a mouse.
You get some words regarding mice,
You get a kitty in a trice.
By two A.M. or thereabout,
The mouse is in, the cat is out.
It dawns upon you, in your cot,
The mouse is silent, the cat is not.
Instead of Pussy, says your spouse,
You should have bought another mouse.

J. R. R. Tolkien
1892-1973

CAT

The fat cat on the mat
    may seem to dream
of nice mice that suffice
    for him, or cream;
but he free, maybe,
    walks in thought
unbowed, proud, where loud
    roared and fought

his kin, lean and slim,
    or deep in den
in the East feasted on beasts
    and tender men.

The giant lion with iron
    claw in paw,
and huge ruthless tooth
    in gory jaw;
the pard dark-starred,
    fleet upon feet,
that oft soft from aloft
    leaps on his meat
where woods loom in gloom—
    far now they be,
    fierce and free,
    and tamed as he;
but fat cat on the mat
    kept as a pet,
    he does not forget.

THE KILKENNY
CATS

There wanst was two cats at Kilkenny,
Each thought there was one cat too many,
    So they quarrell'd and fit,
    They scratched and they bit,
    Till, excepting their nails,
    And the tips of their tails,
Instead of two cats, there warnt any.

Anonymous

A CHILD'S
DISCOVERY

"Oh! it's got pins in its toes!"

36

Paul Gallico
1897-1976

THE BALLAD
OF TOUGH TOM

That's right!
Those are tufts of my fur you're looking at.
What about it?
You don't see the other cat, do you?
What are a few hairs
Compared to an ear?
I didn't get the whole of his off
Because by then he was already heading south,
Having had enough.
But it was eminently satisfactory.
My name is Tough Tom,
And I am King of the Car Park.
When the sun shines
It warms the hoods of the cars for us.
We like that.
We lie on them.
Sometimes we get chased because
We leave footmarks on the cars,
But most of the time nobody bothers,
We have our own crowd that comes here
To sun.
But I say who does and who doesn't.
See?
Because I'm King of the Car Park.
So one day this stranger walks up and says,
"What's your name?"
So I says, "Tough Tom
And I'm King of the Car Park. What's yours?"
And he says, "Tough Charlie, and I guess
You ain't King of the Car Park anymore."
"Oh, I get it," I says, "You're looking for a little
    action."
"How did you guess?" says Tough Charlie.
I'm measuring him up in the meantime
And he's a lot of cat.
Yellow and white.
Yellow is a colour I ain't partial to.
And although I wasn't looking for trouble that
    morning,
Like now by being King of the Car Park,
It was up to me to oblige. So I says,
"Shall we dispense with the preliminaries?
See now, like the growling
And the fluffing
And the humping up

And the exchange of insults?"
Waste of time
When you know you're going to mix.
"Okay by me," says Tough Charlie, "Let's go!"
And he's up and onto me, leading with his right.
Oh boy, a sucker punch.
But I guess I'm a little dopey,
Lying out in that hot sun,
On that warm hood
And maybe he's got a half a pound on me as well.
So I'm on my back before I know it,
And he just misses getting my eye out.
Tough Charlie he was all right.
I give my left on the end of his nose
And try a roll-over
But he's too smart for that
And goes for my eye again, only this time
I'm waiting for it.
He don't get the eye,
But I get his ear.
Brother!
We're all over that car,
Down on the ground,
And underneath,
And back up on top again,
With the gang sitting around
Waiting to see
Who is the King of the Car Park.
He gives me the raking kick
With the back legs.
That's when I lost all that fur
You see about.
But I've still got that ear,
And it's starting to come away.
Tough Tom and Tough Charlie
And the battle of the Car Park!
They'll sing about that one on the tiles
For many a night.
So I guess maybe Tough Charlie thinks it over,
That with only one ear
He ain't gonna do so good anymore
With the broads, and he says,
"Okay, so I was wrong. Leggo!
You're still King of the Car Park."
So I had to laugh, and he's off
With what's left of his ear.
That's the story.
So now for a little clean-up.
I'm still Tough Tom,
King of the Car Park.

The cat, indeed, is the only animal without visible
means of support who still manages to find a living
in the city.   *Carl Van Vechten*

Stephen Vincent Benét

1898-1943

THE KING
OF THE CATS

But, my *dear*," said Mrs Culverin, with a tiny gasp, "you can't actually mean—a *tail!*"

Mrs Dingle nodded impressively. "Exactly. I've seem him. Twice. Paris, of course, and then, a command appearance at Rome—we were in the Royal box. He conducted—my dear, you've never heard such effects from an orchestra—and, my dear," she hesitated slightly, "he conducted *with it.*"

"How perfectly, fascinating too horrid for words!" said Mrs Culverin in a dazed but greedy voice. "We *must* have him to dinner as soon as he come over—he is coming over, isn't he?"

"The twelfth," said Mrs Dingle with a gleam in her eyes. "The New Symphony people have asked him to be guest-conductor for three special concerts —I do hope you can dine with *us* some night while he's here—he'll be very busy, of course—but he's promised to give us what time he can spare—"

"Oh, thank you, dear," said Mrs Culverin, abstractedly, her last raid upon Mrs Dingle's pet British novelist still fresh in her mind. "You're always so delightfully hospitable—but you mustn't wear yourself out—the rest of us must do *our* part—I know Henry and myself would be only too glad to—"

"That's very sweet of you, darling." Mrs Dingle also remembered the larceny of the British novelist. "But we're just going to give Monsieur Tibault— sweet name, isn't it! They say he's descended from the Tybalt in 'Romeo and Juliet' and that's why he doesn't like Shakespeare—we're just going to give Monsieur Tibault the simplest sort of time—a little reception after his first concert perhaps. He hates," she looked around the table, "large, mixed parties. And then, of course, his—er—little idiosyncrasy—" she coughed delicately. "It makes him feel a trifle shy with strangers."

"But I don't understand yet, Aunt Emily," said Tommy Brooks, Mrs Dingle's nephew. "Do you really mean this Tibault bozo has a tail? Like a monkey and everything?"

"Tommy dear," said Mrs Culverin, crushingly, "in the first place, Monsieur Tibault is not a bozo— he is a very distinguished musician—the finest conductor in Europe. And in the second place—"

"He has," Mrs Dingle was firm. "He has a tail. He conducts with it."

"Oh, but honestly!" said Tommy, his ear pinkening. "I mean—of course, if you say so, Aunt Emily, I'm sure he has—but still, it sounds pretty steep, if you know what I mean! How about it, Professor Tatto?"

Professor Tatto cleared his throat. "Tck," he said, putting his fingertips together cautiously, "I shall be very anxious to see this Monsieur Tibault. For myself, I have never observed a genuine specimen of *homo caudatus,* so I should be inclined to doubt, and yet . . . In the Middle Ages, for instance, the belief in men—er—tailed or with caudal appendages of some sort, was both widespread and, as far as we can gather, well founded. As late as the eighteenth century, a Dutch sea-captain with some character for veracity recounts the discovery of a pair of such creatures in the island of Formosa. They were in a low state of civilization, I believe, but the appendages in question were quite distinct. And in 1860, Dr Grimbrook, the English surgeon, claims to have treated no less than three African natives with short but evident tails—though his testimony rests upon his unsupported word. After all, the thing is not impossible, though doubtless unusual. Web feet—rudimentary gills—these occur with some frequency. The appendix we have with us always. The chain of our descent from the ape-like form is by no means complete. For that matter," he beamed around the table, "what can we call the last few vertebrae of the normal spine but the beginnings of a concealed and rudimentary tail? Oh, yes—yes—it's possible—quite—that in an extraordinary case—a reversion of type—a survival—though, of course—"

"I told you so," said Mrs Dingle triumphantly. "*Isn't* it fascinating? Isn't it, Princess?"

The Princess Vivrakananda's eyes, blue as a field of larkspur, fathomless as the centre of heaven, rested lightly for a moment on Mrs Dingle's excited countenance.

"Ve-ry fascinating," she said, in a voice like stroked, golden velvet. "I should like—I should like ve-ry much to meet this Monsier Tibault."

"Well, *I* hope he breaks his neck!" said Tommy Brooks, under his breath—but nobody ever paid much attention to Tommy.

Nevertheless as the time for M Tibault's arrival in these States drew nearer and nearer, people in general began to wonder whether the Princess had spoken quite truthfully—for there was no doubt of the fact that, up till then, she had been the unique sensation of the season—and you know what social lions and lionesses are.

It was, if you remember, a Siamese season, and genuine Siamese were at quite as much of a premium as Russian accents had been in the quaint old days when the Chauve-Souris was a novelty. The Siamese Art Theatre, imported at terrific expense, was playing to packed houses. *Gushuptzgu,* an epic novel of Siamese farm life, in nineteen closely-printed volumes, had just been awarded the Nobel prize. Prominent pet-and-newt dealers reported no cessation in the appalling demand for Siamese cats. And upon the crest of this wave of interest in things Siamese, the Princess Vivrakanarda poised with the elegant nonchalance of a Hawaiian water-baby upon its surfboard. She was indispensable. She was incomparable. She was everywhere.

Youthful, enormously wealthy, allied on one hand to the Royal Family of Siam and on the other to the Cabots (and yet with the first eighteen of her twenty-one years shrouded from speculation in a golden zone of mystery), the mingling of races in her had produced an exotic beauty as distinguished as it was strange. She moved with a feline, effortless grace, and her skin was as if it had been gently powdered with tiny grains of the purest gold—yet the blueness of her eyes, set just a trifle slantingly, was as pure and startling as the sea on the rocks of Maine. Her brown hair fell to her knees—she had been offered extraordinary sums by the Master Barbers' Protective Association to have it shingled. Straight as a waterfall tumbling over brown rocks, it had a vague perfume of sandalwood and suave spices and held tints of rust and the sun. She did not talk very much—but then she did not have to—her voice had an odd, small, melodious huskiness that haunted the mind. She lived alone and was reputed to be very lazy—at least it was known that she slept during most of the day—but at night she bloomed like a moonflower and a depth came into her eyes.

It was no wonder that Tommy Brooks fell in love with her. The wonder was that she let him. There was nothing exotic or distinguished about Tommy —he was just one of those pleasant, normal young men who seem created to carry on the bond business by reading the newspapers in the University Club during most of the day, and can always be relied upon at night to fill an unexpected hole in a dinner-party. It is true that the Princess could hardly be said to do more than tolerate any of her suitors—no one had ever seen those aloofly arrogant eyes enliven at the entrance of any male. But she seemed to be able to tolerate Tommy a little more than the rest—and that young man's infatuated day-dreams were beginning to be beset by smart solitaires and imaginary apartments on Park Avenue, when the famous M Tibault conducted his first concert at Carnegie Hall.

Tommy Brooks sat beside the Princess. The eyes he turned upon her were eyes of longing and love, but her face was as impassive as a mask, and the only remark she made during the preliminary bustlings was that there seemed to be a number of people in the audience. But Tommy was relieved, if anything, to find her even a little more aloof than usual, for, ever since Mrs Culverin's dinner-party, a vague disquiet as to the possible impression which this Tibault creature might make upon her had been growing in his mind. It shows his devotion that he was present at all. To a man whose simple Princetonian nature found in "Just a Little Love, a Little Kiss", the quintessence of musical art, the average symphony was a positive torture, and he looked forward to the evening's programme itself with a grim, brave smile.

"Ssh!" said Mrs Dingle, breathlessly. "He's coming!" It seemed to the startled Tommy as if he were suddenly back in the trenches under a heavy barrage, as M Tibault made his entrance to a perfect bombardment of applause.

Then the enthusiastic noise was sliced off in the middle and a gasp took its place—a vast, windy sigh, as if every person in that multitude had suddenly said, "Ah". For the papers had not lied about him. The tail was there.

They called him theatric—but how well he understood the uses of theatricalism! Dressed in unrelieved black from head to foot (the black dress-shirt had been a special token of Mussolini's esteem), he did not walk on, he strolled, leisurely, easily, aloofly, the famous tail curled nonchalantly about one wrist—a suave, black panther lounging through a summer garden with that little mysterious weave of the head that panthers have when they pad behind bars—the glittering darkness of his eyes unmoved by any surprise or elation. He nodded, twice, in regal acknowledgement, as the clapping reached an apogee of frenzy. To Tommy there was something dreadfully reminiscent of the Princess in the way he nodded. Then he turned to his orchestra.

A second and louder gasp went up from the audience at this point, for, as he turned, the tip of that incredible tail twined with dainty carelessness into some hidden pocket and produced a black baton. But Tommy did not even notice. He was looking at the Princess instead.

She had not even bothered to clap, at first, but now—he had never seen her moved like this, never. She was not applauding, her hands were clenched in her lap, but her whole body was rigid, rigid as a steel bar, and the blue flowers of her eyes were bent upon the figure of M Tibault in a terrible concentration. The pose of her entire figure was so still and intense that for an instant Tommy had the lunatic idea that any moment she might leap from her seat beside him as lightly as a moth, and land, with no sound, at M Tibaut's side to—yes—to rub her proud head against his coat in worship. Even Mrs Dingle would notice in a moment.

"Princess—" he said, in a horrified whisper, "Princess—"

Slowly the tenseness of her body relaxed, her eyes veiled again, she grew calm.

"Yes, Tommy?" she said, in her usual voice, but there was still something about her . . .

"Nothing, only—oh, hang—he's starting!" said Tommy, as M Tibault, his hands loosely clasped before him, turned and *faced* the audience. His eyes dropped, his tail switched once impressively, then gave three little preliminary taps with his baton on the floor.

Seldom has Gluck's overture to "Iphigenie in Aulis" received such an ovation. But it was not until the Eighth Symphony that the hysteria of the audience reached its climax. Never before had the New Symphony played so superbly—and certainly never before had it been led with such genius. Three prominent conductors in the audience were sobbing with the despairing admiration of envious children towards the close, and one at least was heard to offer wildly ten thousand dollars to a well-known facial surgeon there present for a shred of evidence that tails of some variety could by any stretch of science be grafted upon a normally decaudate form. There was no doubt about it—no mortal hand and arm, be they ever so dexterous, could combine the delicate elan and powerful grace displayed in every gesture of M Tibault's tail.

A sable staff, it dominated the brasses like a flicker of black lightning; an ebon, elusive whip, it drew the last exquisite breath of melody from the woodwinds and ruled the stormy strings like a magician's rod. M Tibault bowed and bowed again —roar after roar of frenzied admiration shook the hall to its foundations—and when he finally staggered, exhausted, from the platform, the president of the Wednesday Sonata Club was only restrained by force from flinging her ninety-thousand-dollar string of pearls after him in an excess of aesthetic appreciation. New York had come and seen—and New York was conquered. Mrs Dingle was immediately besieged by reporters, and Tommy Brooks looked forward to the "little party" at which he was to meet the new hero of the hour with feelings only a little less lugubrious than those that would have come to him just before taking his seat in the electric chair.

The meeting between his Princess and M Tibault was worse and better than he expected. Better because, after all, they did not say much to each other —and worse because it seemed to him, somehow, that some curious kinship of mind between them made words unnecessary. They were certainly the most distinguished-looking couple in the room, as he bent over her hand. "So darlingly foreign, both of them, and yet so different," babbled Mrs Dingle —but Tommy couldn't agree.

They were different, yes—the dark, lithe stranger with the bizarre appendage tucked carelessly in his pocket, and the blue-eyed, brown-haired girl. But that difference only accentuated what they had in common—something in the way they moved, in the suavity of their gestures, in the set of their eyes. Something deeper, even, than race. He tried to puzzle it out—then, looking around at the others, he had a flash of revelation. It was as if that couple were foreign, indeed—not only to New York but to all common humanity. As if they were polite guests from a different star.

Tommy did not have a very happy evening, on the whole. But his mind worked slowly, and it was not until much later that the mad suspicion came upon him in full force.

Perhaps he is not to be blamed for his lack of immediate comprehension. The next few weeks were weeks of bewildered misery for him. It was not that the Princess's attitude towards him had changed—she was just as tolerant of him as before, but M Tibault was always there. He had a faculty of appearing, as out of thin air—he walked, for all his height, as lightly as a butterfly—and Tommy grew to hate the faintest shuffle on the carpet that announced his presence.

And then, hang it all, the man was so smooth, so infernally, unruffably smooth! He was never out of temper, never embarrassed. He treated Tommy with the extreme of urbanity, and yet his eyes mocked, deep-down, and Tommy could do nothing. And, gradually, the Princess become more and more drawn to this stranger, in a soundless communion that found little need for speech—and that, too, Tommy saw and hated, and that, too, he could not mend.

He began to be haunted not only by M Tibault in the flesh, but by M Tibault in the spirit. He slept badly, and when he slept, he dreamed—of M Tibault, a man no longer, but a shadow, a spectre, the limber ghost of an animal whose words came purringly between sharp little pointed teeth. There was certainly something odd about the whole shape of the fellow—his fluid ease, the mould of his head, even the cut of his fingernails—but just what it was escaped Tommy's intensest cogitation. And when he did put his finger on it at length, at first he refused to believe.

A pair of petty incidents decided him, finally against all reason. He had gone to Mrs Dingle's, one winter afternoon, hoping to find the Princess. She was out with his aunt, but was expected back for tea, and he wandered idly into the library to wait. He was just about to switch on the lights, for the library was always dark even in summer, when he heard a sound of light breathing that seemed to come from the leather couch in the corner. He approached it cautiously and dimly made out the form of M Tibault, curled up on the couch, peacefully asleep.

The sight annoyed Tommy so that he swore under his breath and was back near the door on his way out, when the feeling we all know and hate, the feeling that eyes we cannot see are watching us, arrested him. He turned back—M Tibault had not moved a muscle of his body to all appearance—but his eyes were open now. And those eyes were black and human no longer. They were green—Tommy could have sworn it—and he could have sworn that they had no bottom and gleamed like little emeralds in the dark. It only lasted a moment, for Tommy pressed the light-button automatically—and there was M Tibault, his normal self, yawning a little but urbanely apologetic, but it gave Tommy time to think. Nor did what happened a trifle later increase his peace of mind.

They had lit a fire and were talking in front of it—by now Tommy hated M Tibault so thoroughly that he felt that odd yearning for his company that often occurs in such cases. M Tibault was telling some anecdote and Tommy was hating him worse than ever for basking with such obvious enjoyment in the heat of the flames and the ripple of his own voice.

Then they heard the street-door open, and M Tibault jumped up—and jumping, caught one sock on a sharp corner of the brass firerail and tore it open in a jagged flap. Tommy looked down mechanically at the tear—a second's glance, but enough—for M Tibault, for the first time in Tommy's experience, lost his temper completely. He swore violently in some spitting, foreign tongue—his face distorted suddenly—he clapped his hand over his sock. Then, glaring furiously at Tommy, he fairly sprang from the room, and Tommy could hear him scaling the stairs in long, agile bounds.

Tommy sank into a chair, careless for once of the fact that he heard the Princess's light laugh in the hall. He didn't want to see the Princess. He didn't want to see anybody. There had been something revealed when M Tibault had torn that hole in his sock—and it was not the skin of a man. Tommy had caught a glimpse of—black plush. Black velvet. And then had come M Tibault's sudden explosion of fury. Good *Lord*—did the man wear black velvet stockings under his ordinary socks? Or could he—could he—but here Tommy held his fevered head in his hands.

He went to Professor Tatto that evening with a series of hypothetical questions, but as he did not dare confide his real suspicions to the Professor, the hypothetical answers he received served only to confuse him the more. Then he thought of Billy Strange. Billy was a good sort, and his mind had a turn for the bizarre. Billy might be able to help.

He couldn't get hold of Billy for three days and lived through the interval in a fever of impatience. But finally they had dinner together at Billy's apartment, where his queer books were, and Tommy was able to blurt out the whole disordered jumble of his suspicions.

Billy listened without interrupting until Tommy was quite through. Then he pulled at his pipe. "But, my dear *man*—" he said, protestingly.

"Oh, I know—I know—" said Tommy, and waved his hands, "I know I'm crazy—you needn't tell me that—but I tell you, the man's a cat all the same—no, I don't see how he could be, but he is—why, hang it, in the first place, everybody knows he's got a tail!"

"Even so," said Billy, puffing. "Oh, my dear Tommy, don't doubt you saw, or think you saw, everything you say. But, even so—" He shook his head.

"But what about those other birds, werewolves and things?" said Tommy.

Billy looked dubious. "We-ll," he admitted, "you've got me there, of course. At least—a tailed man *is* possible. And the yarns about werewolves go back far enough, so that—well, I wouldn't say there aren't or haven't been werewolves—but then I'm willing to believe more things than most people. But a were-cat—or a man that's a cat and a cat that's a man—honestly, Tommy—"

"If I don't get some real advice I'll go clean off my hinge. For Heaven's sake, tell me something to *do*!"

"Lemme think," said Billy. "First, you're pizensure this man is—"

"A cat. Yeah," and Tommy nodded violently.

"Check. And second—if it doesn't hurt your feelings. Tommy—you're afraid this girl you're in love with has—er—at least a streak of—felinity—in her—and so she's drawn to him?"

"Oh, Lord, Billy, if I only knew!"

"Well—er—suppose she really is, too, you know —would you still be keen on her?"

"I'd marry her if she turned into a dragon every Wednesday!" said Tommy, fervently.

Bill smiled. "H'm," he said, "then the obvious thing to do is to get rid of this M Tibault. Lemme think."

He thought about two pipes full, while Tommy sat on pins and needles. Then, finally, he burst out laughing.

"What's so darn funny?" said Tommy, aggrievedly.

"Nothing, Tommy, only I've just thought of a stunt—something so blooming crazy—but if he is —h'm—what you think he is—it *might* work—" And, going to the book-case, he took down a book.

"If you think you're going to quiet my nerves by reading me a bedtime story—"

"Shut up, Tommy, and listen to this—if you really want to get rid of your feline friend."

"What is it?"

"Book of Agnes Repplier's. About cats. Listen."

" 'There is also a Scandinavian version of the ever famous story which Sir Walter Scott told to Washington Irving, which Monk Lewis told to Shelley and which, in one form or another, we find embodied in the folklore of every land'—now, Tommy , pay attention—'the story of the traveller who saw within a ruined abbey, a procession of cats, lowering into a grave a little coffin with a crown upon it. Filled with horror, he hastened from the spot; but when he had reached his destination, he could not forbear relating to a friend the wonder he had seen. Scarcely had the tale been told when his friend's cat, who lay curled up tranquilly by the fire, sprang to its feet, cried out, "Then I am the King of the Cats!" and disappeared in a flash up

the chimney.' "

"Well?" said Billy, shutting the book.

"By gum!" said Tommy, staring. "By gum! Do you think there's a chance?"

"*I* think we're both in the booby-hatch. But if you want to try it—"

"Try it! I'll spring it on him the next time I see him. But—listen—I can't make it a ruined abbey—"

"Oh, use your imagination! Make it Central Park—anywhere. Tell it as if it happened to you— seeing the funeral procession and all that. You can lead into it somehow—let's see—some general line —oh, yes—'Strange, isn't it, how fact so often copies fiction. Why, only yesterday—' See?"

"Strange, isn't it, how fact so often copies fiction," repeated Tommy dutifully. "Why, only yesterday—"

"I happened to be strolling through Central Park when I saw something very odd."

"I happened to be strolling through—here, gimme that book!" said Tommy, "I want to learn the rest of it by heart!"

Mrs Dingle's farewell dinner to the famous Monsieur Tibault, on the occasion of his departure for his Western tour, was looked forward to with the greatest expectations. Not only would everybody be there, including the Princess Vivrakanarda, but Mrs Dingle, a hinter if there ever was one, had let it be known that at this dinner an announcement of very unusual interest to Society might be made. So everyone, for once, was almost on time, except for Tommy. He was at least fifteen minutes early, for he wanted to have speech with his aunt alone. Unfortunately, however, he had hardly taken off his overcoat when she was whispering some news in his ear so rapidly that he found it difficult to understand a word of it.

"And you mustn't breathe it to a soul!" she ended, beaming. "That is, not before the announcement—I think we'll have *that* with the salad—people never pay very much attention to salad—"

"Breathe what, Aunt Emily?" said Tommy, confused.

"The Princess, darling—the dear Princess and Monsieur Tibault—they just got engaged this afternoon, dear things! Isn't it *fascinating*?"

"Yeah," said Tommy, and started to walk blindly through the nearest door. His aunt restrained him.

"Not there, dear—not in the library. You can congratulate them later. They're just having a sweet little moment alone there now—" And she turned away to harry the butler, leaving Tommy stunned.

But his chin came up after a moment. He wasn't beaten yet.

"Strange, isn't it, how often fact copies fiction?" he repeated to himself in dull mnemonics, and, as he did so, he shook his fist at the library door.

Mrs Dingle was wrong, as usual. The Princess and M Tibault were not in the library—they were in the conservatory, as Tommy discovered when he wandered aimlessly past the glass doors.

He didn't mean to look, and after a second he turned away. But that second was enough.

Tibault was seated in a chair and she was crouched on a stool at his side, while his hand, softly, smoothly, stroked her brown hair. Black cat and Siamese kitten. Her face was hidden from Tommy, but he could see Tibault's face. And he could hear.

They were not talking, but there was a sound between them. A warm and contented sound like the murmur of giant bees in a hollow tree—a golden, musical rumble, deep-throated, that came from Tibault's lips and answered by hers—a golden purr.

Tommy found himself back in the drawing-room, shaking hands with Mrs Culverin, who said, frankly, that she had seldom seen him look so pale.

The first two courses of the dinner passed Tommy like dreams, but Mrs Dingle's cellar was notable, and by the middle of the meat course, he began to come to himself. He had only one resolve now.

For the next few moments he tried desperately to break into the conversation, but Mrs Dingle was talking, and even Gabriel will have a time interrupting Mrs Dingle. At last, though, she paused for breath and Tommy saw his chance.

"Speaking of that," said Tommy, piercingly, without knowing in the least what he was referring to, "Speaking of that—"

"As I was saying," said Professor Tatto. But Tommy would not yield. The plates were being taken away. It was time for salad.

"Speaking of that," he said again, so loudly and strangely that Mrs Culverin jumped and an awkward hush fell over the table. "Strange, isn't it, how often fact copies fiction?" There, he was startled. His voice rose even higher. "Why, only today I was strolling through—" and, word for word, he repeated his lesson. He could see Tibault's eyes glowing at him, as he described the funeral. He could see the Princess, tense.

He could not have said what he had expected might happen when he came to the end; but it was not bored silence, everywhere, to be followed by Mrs Dingle's acrid, "Well, Tommy, is that *quite*

all?"

He slumped back in his chair, sick at heart. He was a fool and his last resource had failed. Dimly he heard his aunt's voice, saying, "Well, then—" and realized that she was about to make the fatal announcement.

But just then Monsieur Tibault spoke.

"One moment, Mrs Dingle," he said, with extreme politeness, and she was silent. He turned to Tommy.

"You are—positive I suppose, of what you saw this afternoon, Brooks?" he said, in tones of light mockery.

"Absolutely," said Tommy sullenly. "Do you think I'd—"

"Oh, no, no, no," Monsieur Tibault waved the implication aside, "but—such an interesting story —one likes to be sure of the details—and, of course, you *are* sure—*quite* sure—that the kind of crown you describe was on the coffin?"

"Of course," said Tommy, wondering, "but—"

"Then I'm the King of the Cats!" cried Monsieur Tibault in a voice of thunder, and, even as he cried it, the houselights blinked—there was the soft thud of an explosion that seemed muffled in cotton-wool from the minstrel gallery—and the scene was lit for a second by an obliterating and painful burst of light that vanished in an instant and was succeeded by heavy, blinding clouds of white, pungent smoke.

"Oh, those *horrid* photographers," came Mrs Dingle's voice in a melodious wail. "I *told* them not to take the flashlight picture till dinner was over, and now they've taken it *just* as I was nibbling lettuce!"

Someone tittered a little nervously. Someone coughed. Then, gradually the veils of smoke dislimned and the green-and-black spots in front of Tommy's eyes died away.

They were blinking at each other like people who have just come out of a cave into brilliant sun. Even yet their eyes stung with the fierceness of that abrupt illumination and Tommy found it hard to make out the faces across the table from him.

Mrs Dingle took command of the half-blinded company with her accustomed poise. She rose, glass in hand. "And now, dear friends," she said in a clear voice, "I'm sure all of us are very happy to—" Then she stopped, open-mouthed, an expression of incredulous horror on her features. The lifted glass began to spill its contents on the tablecloth in a little stream of amber. As she spoke, she had turned directly to Monsieur Tibault's place at the table—and Monsieur Tibault was no longer there.

Some say there was a bursting flash of fire that disappeared up the chimney—some say it was a giant cat that leaped through the window at a bound, without breaking the glass. Professor Tatto puts it down to a mysterious chemical disturbance operating only over M Tibault's chair. The butler, who is pious, believes the devil in person flew away with him, and Mrs Dingle hesitates between witch-craft and a malicious ectoplasm dematerializing on the wrong cosmic plane. But be that as it may, one thing is certain—in the instant of fictive darkness which followed the glare of the flashlight, Monsieur Tibault, the great conductor, disappeared forever from mortal sight, tail and all.

Mrs Culverin swears he was an international burglar and that she was just about to unmask him, when he slipped away under cover of the flashlight smoke, but no one else who sat at that historic dinner-table believes her. No, there are no sound explanations, but Tommy thinks he knows, and he will never be able to pass a cat again without wondering.

Mrs Tommy is quite of her husband's mind regarding cats—she was Gretchen Woolwine, of Chicago—for Tommy told her his whole story, and while she doesn't believe a great deal of it, there is no doubt in her heart that one person concerned in the affair was a *perfect* cat. Doubtless it would have been more romantic to relate how Tommy's daring finally won him his Princess—but, unfortunately, it would not be veracious. For the Princess Vivrakanarda, also, is with us no longer. Her nerves, shattered by the spectacular denouement of Mrs Dingle's dinner, required a sea-voyage, and from that voyage she has never returned to America.

Of course, there are the usual stories—one hears of her, a nun in a Siamese convent, or a masked dancer at Le Jardin de ma Soeur—one hears that she has been murdered in Patagonia or married in Trebizond—but, as far as can be ascertained, not one of these gaudy fables has the slightest basis of fact. I believe that Tommy, in his heart of hearts, is quite convinced that the sea-voyage was only a pretext, and that by some unheard-of means, she has managed to rejoin the formidable Monsieur Tibault, wherever in the world of the visible or the invisible he may be—in fact, that in some ruined city or subterranean palace they reign together now, King and Queen of all the mysterious Kingdom of Cats. But that, of course, is quite impossible.

Ah! cats are a mysterious kind of folk. There is more passing in their minds than we are aware of.
Sir Walter Scott

A. B. Mitford (Lord Redesdale)
1837-1916

THE VAMPIRE
CAT OF
NABESHIMA

There is a tradition in the Nabéshima family that, many years ago, the Prince of Hizen was bewitched and cursed by a cat that had been kept by one of his retainers. This prince had in his house a lady of rare beauty, called O Toyo: amongst all his ladies she was the favourite, and there was none who could rival her charms and accomplishments. One day the Prince went out into the garden with O Toyo, and remained enjoying the fragrance of the flowers until sunset, when they returned to the palace, never noticing that they were being followed by a large cat. Having parted with her lord, O Toyo retired to her own room and went to bed. At midnight she awoke with a start, and became aware of a huge cat that crouched watching her; and when she cried out, the beast sprang on her, and fixing its cruel teeth in her delicate throat, throttled her to death. What a piteous end for so fair a dame, the darling of her prince's heart, to die suddenly, bitten to death by a cat! Then the cat, having scratched out a grave under the verandah, buried the corpse of O Toyo, and assuming her form, began to bewitch the Prince.

But my lord the Prince knew nothing of all this, and little thought that the beautiful creature who caressed and fondled him was an impish and foul beast that had slain his mistress and assumed her shape in order to drain out his life's blood. Day by day, as time went on, the Prince's strength dwindled away; the colour of his face was changed, and became pale and livid; and he was as a man suffering from a deadly sickness. Seeing this, his councillors and his wife became greatly alarmed, so they summoned the physicians, who prescribed various remedies for him; but the more medicine he took, the more serious did his illness appear, and no treatment was of any avail. But most of all did he suffer in the night-time, when his sleep would be troubled and disturbed by hideous dreams. In consequence of this, his councillors nightly appointed a hundred of his retainers to sit up and watch over him; but, strange to say, towards ten o'clock on the very first night that the watch was set, the guard were seized with a sudden and unaccountable drowsiness, which they could not resist, until one by one every man had fallen asleep. Then the false O Toyo came in and harassed the Prince until morning. The following night the same thing occurred, and the Prince was subjected to the imp's tyranny, while his guards slept helplessly around him. Night after night this was repeated, until at last three of the Prince's councillors determined themselves to sit up on guard, and see whether they could overcome this mysterious drowsiness, but they fared no better than the others, and by ten o'clock were fast asleep. The next day the three councillors held a solemn conclave, and their chief, one Isahaya Buzen, said—

"This is a marvellous thing, that a guard of a hundred men should thus be overcome by sleep. Of a surety, the spell that is upon my lord and upon his guard must be the work of witchcraft. Now, as all our efforts are of no avail, let us seek out Ruiten, the chief priest of the temple called Miyo In, and beseech him to put up prayers for the recovery of my lord."

And the other councillors approving what Isahaya Buzen had said, they went to the priest Ruiten and engaged him to recite litanies that the Prince might be restored to health.

So it came to pass that Ruiten, the chief priest of Miyo In, offered up prayers nightly for the Prince. One night, at the ninth hour (midnight), when he had finished his religious exercises and was preparing to lie down to sleep, he fancied that he heard a noise outside in the garden, as if some one were washing himself at the well. Deeming this passing strange, he looked down from the window; and there in the moonlight he saw a handsome young soldier, some twenty-four years of age, washing himself, who, when he had finished cleaning himself and had put on his clothes, stood before the figure of Buddha and prayed fervently for the recovery of my lord the Prince. Ruiten looked on with admiration; and the young man, when he had made an end of his prayer, was going away; but the priest stopped him, calling out to him—

"Sir, I pray you to tarry a little: I have something to say to you."

"At your reverence's service. What may you please to want?"

"Pray be so good as to step up here, and have a little talk."

"By your reverence's leave;" and with this he went upstairs.

Then Ruiten said—

"Sir, I cannot conceal my admiration that you, being so young a man, should have so loyal a spirit. I am Ruiten , the chief priest of this temple, who am engaged in praying for the recovery of my lord. Pray what is your name?"

"My name, sir, is Ito Soda, and I am serving in the infantry of Nabéshima. Since my lord has been sick, my one desire has been to assist in nursing him; but, being only a simple soldier, I am not of sufficient rank to come into his presence, so I have no resource but to pray to the gods of the country and to Buddha that my lord may regain his health."

When Ruiten heard this, he shed tears in admiration of the fidelity of Ito Soda, and said—

"Your purpose is, indeed, a good one; but what a strange sickness this is that my lord is afflicted with! Every night he suffers from horrible dreams; and the retainers who sit up with him are all seized with a mysterious sleep, so that not one can keep awake. It is very wonderful."

"Yes," replied Soda, after a moment's reflection, "this certainly must be witchcraft. If I could but obtain leave to sit up one night with the Prince, I would fain see whether I could not resist this drowsiness and detect the goblin."

At last the priest said, "I am in relations of friendship with Isahaya Buzen, the chief councillor of the Prince. I will speak to him of you and of your loyalty, and will intercede with him that you may attain your wish."

"Indeed, sir I am most thankful. I am not prompted by any vain thought of self-advancement, should I succeed: all I wish for is the recovery of my lord. I commend myself to your kind favour."

"'Well, then, to-morrow night I will take you with me to the councillor's house."

"Thank you, sir, and farewell." And so they parted.

On the following evening Ito Soda returned to the temple Miyo In, and having found Ruiten, accompanied him to the house of Isahaya Buzen: then the priest, leaving Soda outside, went in to converse with the councillor, and inquire after the Prince's health.

"And pray, sir, how is my lord? Is he in any better condition since I have been offering up prayers for him?"

"Indeed, no; his illness is very severe. We are certain that he must be the victim of some foul sorcery; but as there are no means of keeping a guard awake after ten o'clock, we cannot catch a sight of the goblin, so we are in the greatest trouble."

"I feel deeply for you: it must be most distressing. However, I have something to tell you. I think that I have found a man who will detect the goblin; and I have brought him with me."

"Indeed! who is the man?"

"Well, he is one of my lord's foot-soldiers, named Ito Soda, a faithful fellow, and I trust that you will grant his request to be permitted to sit up with my lord."

"Certainly, it is wonderful to find so much loyalty and zeal in a common soldier," replied Isahaya Buzen, after a moment's reflection; "still it is impossible to allow a man of such low rank to perform the office of watching over my lord."

"It is true that he is but a common soldier," urged the priest; "but why not raise his rank in consideration of his fidelity, and then let him mount guard?"

"It would be time enough to promote him after my lord's recovery. But come, let me see this Ito Soda, that I may know what manner of man he is: if he pleases me, I will consult with the other councillors, and perhaps we may grant his request."

"I will bring him in forthwith," replied Ruiten, who thereupon went out to fetch the young man.

When he returned, the priest presented Ito Soda to the councillor, who looked at him attentively, and, being pleased with his comely and gentle appearance, said—

"So I hear that you are anxious to be permitted to mount guard in my lord's room at night. Well, I must consult with the other councillors, and we will see what can be done for you."

When the young soldier heard this he was greatly elated, and took his leave, after warmly thanking Ruiten, who had helped him to gain his object. The next day the councillors held a meeting, and sent for Ito Soda, and told him that he might keep watch with the other retainers that very night. So he went his way in high spirits, and at nightfall, having made all his preparations, took his place among the hundred gentlemen who were on duty in the prince's bed-room.

Now the Prince slept in the centre of the room, and the hundred guards around him sat keeping themselves awake with entertaining conversation and pleasant conceits. But, as ten o'clock approached, they began to doze off as they sat; and in spite of all their endeavours to keep one another awake, by degrees they all fell asleep. Ito Soda all this while felt an irresistible desire to sleep creeping over him, and, though he tried by all sorts of ways to rouse himself, he saw that there was no help for it, but by resorting to an extreme measure, for which he had already made his preparations. Drawing out a piece of oil paper which he had brought with him, and spreading it over the mats, he sat down upon it; then he took the small knife which he carried in the sheath of his dirk, and stuck it into his own thigh. For awhile the pain of the wound kept him awake; but as the slumber by which he was assailed was the work of sorcery, little by little he became drowsy again. Then he twisted the knife round and round in his thigh, so that the pain becoming very violent, he was proof against the feeling of sleepiness, and kept a faithful watch. Now the oil paper which he had spread under his legs was in order to prevent the blood, which might spurt from his wound, from defiling the mats.

So Ito Soda remained awake, but the rest of the guard slept; and as he watched, suddenly the sliding-doors of the Prince's room were drawn open, and he saw a figure coming in stealthily, and, as it drew nearer, the form was that of a marvellously beautiful woman some twenty-three years of age. Cautiously she looked around her; and when she saw that all the guard were asleep, she smiled an ominous smile, and was going up to the Prince's bedside, when she perceived that in one corner of the room there was a man yet awake. This seemed to startle her, but she went up to Soda and said—

"I am not used to seeing you here. Who are you?"

"My name is Ito Soda, and this is the first night that I have been on guard."

"A troublesome office, truly! Why, here are all the rest of the guard asleep. How is it that you alone are awake? You are a trusty watchman."

"There is nothing to boast about. I'm asleep myself, fast and sound."

"What is that wound on your knee? It is all red with blood."

"Oh! I felt very sleepy; so I stuck my knife into my thigh, and the pain of it has kept me awake."

"What wondrous loyalty!" said the lady.

"Is it not the duty of a retainer to lay down his life for his master? Is such a scratch as this worth thinking about?"

Then the lady went up to the sleeping prince and said, "How fares it with my lord to-night?" But the Prince, worn out with sickness, made no reply. But Soda was watching her eagerly, and guessed that it was O Toyo, and made up his mind that if she attempted to harass the Prince he would kill her on the spot. The goblin, however, which in the form of O Toyo had been tormenting the Prince every night, and had come again that night for no other purpose, was defeated by the watchfulness of Ito Soda; for whenever she drew near to the sick man, thinking to put her spells upon him, she would turn and look behind her, and there she saw Ito Soda glaring at her; so she had no help for it but to go away again, and leave the Prince undisturbed.

At last the day broke, and the other officers, when they awoke and opened their eyes, saw that Ito Soda had kept awake by stabbing himself in the thigh; and they were greatly ashamed and went home crestfallen.

That morning Ito Soda went to the house of Isahaya Buzen, and told him all that had occurred the previous night. The councillors were all loud in their praise of Ito Soda's behaviour, and ordered him to keep watch again that night. At the same hour, the false O Toyo came and looked all round the room, and all the guard were asleep, excepting Ito Soda, who was wide awake; and so, being again frustrated, she returned to her own apartments.

Now as since Soda had been on guard the Prince had passed quiet nights, his sickness began to get better, and there was great joy in the palace, and Soda was promoted and rewarded with an estate. In the meanwhile O Toyo, seeing that her nightly visits bore no fruits, kept away; and from that time forth the night-guard were no longer subject to fits of drowsiness. This coincidence struck Soda as very strange, so he went to Isahaya Buzen and told him that of a certainty this O Toyo was no other than a goblin. Isahaya Buzen reflected for a while, and said—

"Well, then, how shall we kill the foul thing?"

"I will go to creature's room, as if nothing were the matter, and try to kill her; but in case she should try to escape, I will beg you to order eight men to stop outside and lie in wait for her."

Having agreed upon this plan, Soda went at nightfall to O Toyo's apartment, pretending to have been sent with a message from the Prince. When she saw him arrive, she said—

"What message have you brought me from my lord?"

"Oh! nothing in particular. Be so good as to look at this letter;" and as he spoke, he drew near to her, and suddenly drawing his dirk cut at her; but the goblin, springing back, seized a halberd, and glaring fiercely at Soda, said—

"How dare you behave like this to one of your

lord's ladies? I will have you dismissed;" and she tried to strike Soda with the halberd. But Soda fought desperately with his dirk; and the goblin, seeing that she was no match for him, threw away the halberd, and from a beautiful woman became suddenly transformed into a cat, which, springing up the sides of the room, jumped on to the roof. Isahaya Buzen and his eight men who were watching outside shot at the cat, but missed it, and the beast made good its escape.

So the cat fled to the mountains, and did much mischief among the surrounding people, until at last the Prince of Hizen ordered a great hunt; and the beast was killed.

But the Prince recovered from his sickness; and Ito Soda was richly rewarded.

Edgar Allan Poe

1809-1849

THE BLACK CAT

For the most wild, yet most homely narrative which I am about to pen, I neither expect nor solicit belief. Mad indeed would I be to expect it, in a case where my very senses reject their own evidence. Yet, mad am I not—and very surely do I not dream. But tomorrow I die, and to-day I would unburthen my soul. My immediate purpose is to place before the world, plainly, succinctly, and without comment, a series of mere household events. In their consequences, these events have terrified—have tortured—have destroyed me. Yet I will not attempt to expound them. To me, they have presented little but Horror —to many they will seem less terrible than *baroques*. Hereafter, perhaps, some intellect may be found which will reduce my phantasm to the common-place—some intellect more calm, more logical, and far less excitable than my own, which will perceive, in the circumstances I detail with awe, nothing more than an ordinary succession of very natural causes and effects.

From my infancy I was noted for the docility and humanity of my disposition. My tenderness of heart was even so conspicuous as to make me the jest of my companions. I was especially fond of animals, and was indulged by my parents with a great variety of pets. With these I spent most of my time, and never was so happy as when feeding and caressing them. This peculiarity of character grew with my growth, and, in my manhood, I derived from it one of my principal sources of pleasure. To those who have cherished an affection for a faithful and sagacious dog, I need hardly be at the trouble of explaining the nature or the intensity of the gratification thus derivable. There is something in the unselfish and self-sacrificing love of a brute, which goes directly to the heart of him who has had frequent occasion to test the paltry friendship and gossamer fidelity of mere *Man*.

I married early, and was happy to find in my wife a disposition not uncongenial with my own. Observing my partiality for domestic pets, she lost no opportunity of procuring those of the most agreeable kind. We had birds, gold fish, a fine dog, rabbits, a small monkey, and *a cat*.

This latter was a remarkably large and beautiful animal, entirely black, and sagacious to an astonishing degree. In speaking of his intelligence, my wife, who at heart was not a little tinctured with superstition, made frequent allusion to the ancient popular notion, which regarded all black cats as witches in disguise. Not that she was ever *serious* upon this point—and I mention the matter at all for no better reason than that it happens, just now, to be remembered.

Pluto—this was the cat's name—was my favorite pet and playmate. I alone fed him, and he attended me wherever I went about the house. It was even with difficulty that I could prevent him from following me through the streets.

Our friendship lasted, in this manner, for several years, during which my general temperament and character—through the instrumentality of the Fiend Intemperance—had (I blush to confess it) experienced a radical alteration for the worse. I grew, day by day, more moody, more irritable, more regardless of the feelings of others. I suffered myself to use intemperate language to my wife. At length, I even offered her personal violence. My pets, of course, were made to feel the change in my disposition. I not only neglected, but ill-used them. For Pluto, however, I still retained sufficient regard to restrain me from maltreating him, as I made no scruple of maltreating the rabbits, the monkey, or even the dog, when by accident, or through affection, they came in my way. But my disease grew upon me—for what disease is like Alcohol!—and at length even Pluto, who was now becoming old, and consequently somewhat peevish—even Pluto began to experience the effects of my ill temper.

One night, returning home, much intoxicated, from one of my haunts about town, I fancied that the cat avoided my presence. I seized him; when, in his fright at my violence, he inflicted a slight wound upon my hand with his teeth. The fury of a demon instantly possessed me. I knew myself no longer. My original soul seemed, at once, to take its flight from my body; and a more than fiendish mal-evolence, gin-nurtured, thrilled every fibre of my frame. I took from my waistcoat-pocket a pen-knife, opened it, grasped the poor beast by the throat, and deliberately cut one of its eyes from the socket! I blush, I burn, I shudder, while I pen the damnable atrocity.

When reason returned with the morning—when I had slept off the fumes of the night's debauch—I experienced a sentiment half of horror, half of re-morse, for the crime of which I had been guilty; but it was, at best, a feeble and equivocal feeling, and the soul remained untouched; I again plunged into

excess, and soon drowned in wine all memory of the deed.

In the meantime the cat slowly recovered. The socket of the lost eye presented, it is true, a frightful appearance, but he no longer appeared to suffer any pain. He went about the house as usual, but, as might be expected, fled in extreme terror at my approach. I had so much of my old heart left, as to be at first grieved by this evident dislike on the part of a creature which had once so loved me. But this feeling soon gave place to irritation. And then came, as if to my final and irrevocable overthrow, the spirit of PERVERSENESS. Of this spirit philosophy takes no account. Yet I am not more sure that my soul lives, than I am that perverseness is one of the primitive impulses of the human heart—one of the indivisible primary faculties, or sentiments, which give direction to the character of Man. Who has not, a hundred times, found himself committing a vile or a silly action, for no other reason than because he knows he should *not?* Have we not a perpetual inclination, in the teeth of our best judgment, to violate that which is *Law,* merely because we understand it to be such? This spirit of perverse-

ness, I say, came to my final overthrow. It was this unfathomable longing of the soul *to vex itself*—to offer violence to its own nature—to do wrong for the wrong's sake only—that urged me to continue and finally to consummate the injury I had inflicted upon the unoffending brute. One morning, in cool blood, I slipped a noose about its neck and hung it to the limb of a tree;—hung it with the tears streaming from my eyes, and with the bitterest remorse at my heart;—hung it *because* I knew that it had loved me, and *because* I felt it had given me no reason of offence;—hung it *because* I knew that in so doing I was committing a sin—a deadly sin that would so jeopardize my immortal soul as to place it— if such a thing were possible—even beyond the reach of the infinite mercy of the Most Merciful and Most Terrible God.

On the night of the day on which this cruel deed was done, I was aroused from sleep by the cry of fire. The curtains of my bed were in flames. The whole house was blazing. It was with great difficulty that my wife, a servant, and myself, made our escape from the conflagration. The destruction was complete. My entire worldly wealth was swallowed up, and I resigned myself thenceforward to despair.

I am above the weakness of seeking to establish a sequence of cause and effect, between the disaster and the atrocity. But I am detailing a chain of facts—and wish not to leave even a possible link imperfect. On the day succeeding the fire, I visited the ruins. The walls, with one exception, had fallen in. This exception was found in a compartment wall, not very thick, which stood about the middle of the house, and against which had rested the head of my bed. The plastering had here, in great measure, resisted the action of the fire—a fact which I attributed to its having been recently spread. About this wall a dense crowd were collected, and many persons seemed to be examining a particular portion of it with very minute and eager attention. The words "strange!" "singular!" and other similar expressions, excited my curiosity. I approached and saw, as if graven in *bas relief* upon the white surface, the figure of a gigantic *cat*. The impression was given with an accuracy truly marvelous. There was a rope about the animal's neck.

When I first beheld this apparition—for I could scarcely regard it as less—my wonder and my terror were extreme. But at length reflection came to my aid. The cat, I remembered, had been hung in a garden adjacent to the house. Upon the alarm of fire, this garden had been immediately filled by the crowd—by some one of whom the animal must have been cut from the tree and thrown, through an open window, into my chamber. This had probably been done with the view of arousing me from sleep. The falling of other walls had compressed the victim of my cruelty into the substance of the freshly-spread plaster; the lime of which, with the flames, and the *ammonia* from the carcass, had then accomplished the portraiture as I saw it.

Although I thus readily accounted to my reason, if not altogether to my conscience, for the startling fact just detailed, it did not the less fail to make a deep impression upon my fancy. For months I could not rid myself of the phantasm of the cat; and, during this period, there came back into my spirit a half-sentiment that seemed, but was not, remorse. I went so far as to regret the loss of the animal, and to look about me, among the vile haunts which I now habitually frequented, for another pet of the same species, and of somewhat similar appearance, with which to supply its place.

One night as I sat, half stupified, in a den of more than infamy, my attention was suddenly drawn to some black object, reposing upon the head of one of the immense hogsheads of Gin, or of Rum, which constituted the chief furniture of the apartment. I had been looking steadily at the top of this hogshead for some minutes, and what now caused me surprise was the fact that I had not sooner perceived the object thereupon. I approached it, and touched it with my hand. It was a black cat—a very large one—fully as large as Pluto, and closely resembling him in every respect but one. Pluto had not a white hair upon any portion of his body; but this cat had a large, although indefinite splotch of white, covering nearly the whole region of the breast.

Upon my touching him, he immediately arose, purred loudly, rubbed against my hand, and appeared delighted with my notice. This, then, was the very creature of which I was in search. I at once offered to purchase it of the landlord; but this person made no claim to it—knew nothing of it—had never seen it before.

I continued my caresses, and, when I prepared to go home, the animal evinced a disposition to accompany me. I permitted it to do so; occasionally stooping and patting it as I proceeded. When it reached the house it domesticated itself at once, and became immediately a great favorite with my wife.

For my own part, I soon found a dislike to it arising within me. This was just the reverse of what I had anticipated; but I know not how or why it was—its evident fondness for myself rather disgusted and annoyed. By slow degrees, these feelings of disgust and annoyance rose into the bitterness of hatred. I avoided the creature; a certain sense of shame, and the remembrance of my former deed of cruelty, preventing me from physically abusing it. I did not, for some weeks, strike, or otherwise violently ill use it; but gradually—very gradually—I came to look upon it with unutterable loathing, and to flee silently from its odious presence, as from the breath of a pestilence.

What added, no doubt, to my hatred of the beast, was the discovery, on the morning after I brought it home, that, like Pluto, it also had been deprived of one of its eyes. This circumstance, however, only endeared it to my wife, who, as I have already said, possessed, in a high degree, that humanity of feeling which had once been my distinguishing trait, and the source of many of my simplest and purest pleasures.

With my aversion to this cat, however, its partiality for myself seemed to increase. It followed my footsteps with a pertinacity which it would be difficult to make the reader comprehend. Whenever I sat, it would crouch beneath my chair, or spring upon my knees, covering me with its loathsome caresses. If I arose to walk it would get between my feet and thus nearly throw me down, or, fastening its long and sharp claws in my dress, clamber, in this manner, to my breast. At such times, although I longed to destroy it with a blow, I was yet withheld from so doing, partly by a memeory of my former crime, but chiefly—let me confess it at once—by absolute *dread* of the beast.

This dread was not exactly a dread of physical evil—and yet I should be at a loss how otherwise to define it. I am almost ashamed to own—yes, even in this felon's cell, I am almost ashamed to own—that the terror and horror with which the animal inspired me, had been heightened by one of the merest chimaeras it would be possible to conceive. My wife had called my attention, more than once, to the character of the mark of white hair, of which I have spoken, and which constituted the sole visible difference between the strange beast and the one I had destroyed. The reader will remember that this mark, although large, had been originally very indefinite; but, by slow degrees—degrees nearly imperceptible, and which for a long time my Reason struggled to reject as fanciful—it had, at length, assumed a rigorous distinctness of outline. It was now the representation of an object that I shudder to name—and for this, above all, I loathed, and dreaded, and would have rid myself of the monster *had I dared*—it was now, I say, the image of a hideous—of a ghastly thing—of the Gallows!—

oh, mournful and terrible engine of Horror and of Crime—of Agony and of Death!

And now was I indeed wretched beyond the wretchedness of mere Humanity. And *a brute beast*—whose fellow I had contemptuously destroyed—*a brute beast* to work out for *me*—for me a man, fashioned in the image of the High God—so much of insufferable wo! Alas! neither by day nor by night knew I the blessing of Rest any more! During the former the creature left me no moment alone; and, in the latter, I started, hourly, from dreams of unutterable fear, to find the hot breath of *the thing* upon my face, and its vast weight—an incarnate Night-Mare that I had no power to shake off—incumbent eternally upon my *heart!*

Beneath the pressure of torments such as these, the feeble remnant of the good within me succumbed. Evil thoughts became my sole intimates—the darkest and most evil of thoughts. The moodiness of my usual temper increased to hatred of all things and of all mankind; while, from the sudden, frequent, and ungovernable outbursts of a fury to which I now blindly abandoned myself, my uncomplaining wife, alas! was the most usual and the most patient of sufferers.

One day she accompanied me, upon some household errand, into the cellar of the old building which our poverty compelled us to inhabit. The cat followed me down the steep stairs, and, nearly throwing me headlong, exasperated me to madness. Uplifting an axe, and forgetting, in my wrath, the childish dread which had hitherto stayed my hand, I aimed a blow at the animal which, of course, would have proved instantly fatal had it descended as I wished. But this blow was arrested by the hand of my wife. Goaded, by the interference, into a rage more than demoniacal, I withdrew my arm from her grasp and buried the axe in her brain. She fell dead upon the spot, without a groan.

This hideous murder accomplished, I set myself forthwith, and with entire deliberation, to the task of concealing the body. I knew that I could not remove it from the house, either by day or by night, without the risk of being observed by the neighbors. Many projects entered my mind. At one period I thought of cutting the corpse into minute fragments, and destroying them by fire. At another, I resolved to dig a grave for it in the floor of the cellar. Again, I deliberated about casting it in the well in the yard—about packing it in a box, as if merchandize, with the usual arrangements, and so getting a porter to take it from the house. Finally I hit upon what I considered a far better expedient than either of these. I determined to wall it up in the cellar—as the monks of the middle ages are recorded to have walled up their victims.

For a purpose such as this the cellar was well adapted. Its walls were loosely constructed, and had lately been plastered throughout with a rough plaster, which the dampness of the atmosphere had prevented from hardening. Moreover, in one of the walls was a projection, caused by a false chimney, or fireplace, that had been filled up, and made to resemble the rest of the cellar. I made no doubt that I could readily displace the bricks at this point, insert the corpse, and wall the whole up as before, so that no eye could detect anything suspicious.

And in this calculation I was not deceived. By means of a crow-bar I easily dislodged the bricks, and, having carefully deposited the body against the inner wall, I propped it in that position, while, with little trouble, I re-laid the whole structure as it originally stood. Having procured mortar, sand, and hair, with every possible precaution, I prepared a plaster which could not be distinguished from the old, and with this I very carefully went over the new brick-work. When I had finished, I felt satisfied that all was right. The wall did not present the slightest appearance of having been disturbed. The rubbish on the floor was picked up with the minutest care. I looked around triumphantly, and said to myself—"Here at least, then, my labor has not been in vain."

My next step was to look for the beast which had been the cause of so much wretchedness; for I had, at length, firmly resolved to put it to death. Had I been able to meet with it, at the moment, there could have been no doubt of its fate; but it appeared that the crafty animal had been alarmed at the violence of my previous anger, and forebore to present itself in my present mood. It is impossible to describe, or to imagine, the deep, the blissful sense of relief which the absence of the detested creature occasioned in my bosom. It did not make its appearance during the night—and thus for one night at least, since its introduction into the house, I soundly and tranquilly slept; aye, *slept* even with the burden of murder upon my soul!

The second and the third day passed, and still my tormentor came not. Once again I breathed as a free-man. The monster, in terror, had fled the premises forever! I should behold it no more! My happiness was supreme! The guilt of my dark deed disturbed me but little. Some few inquiries had been made, but these had been readily answered. Even a search had been instituted—but of course nothing was to be discovered. I looked upon my future felicity as secured.

Upon the fourth day of the assassination, a party of the police came, very unexpectedly, into the house, and proceeded again to make rigorous investigation of the premises. Secure, however, in the inscrutability of my place of concealment, I felt no embarrassment whatever. The officers bade me accompany them in their search. They left no nook or corner unexplored. At length, for the third or fourth time, they descended into the cellar. I quivered not a muscle. My heart beat calmly as that of one who slumbers in innocence. I walked the cellar from end to end. I folded my arms upon my bosom, and roamed easily to and fro. The police were thoroughly satisfied and prepared to depart. The glee at my heart was too strong to be restrained. I burned to say if but one word, by way of triumph, and to render doubly sure their assurance of my guiltlessness.

"Gentlemen," I said at last, as the party ascended the steps, "I delight to have allayed your suspicions. I wish you all health, and a little more courtesy. By the bye, gentlemen, this—this is a very well constructed house." [In the rabid desire to say something easily, I scarcely knew what I uttered at all.]—"I may say an *excellently* well constructed house. These walls—are you going, gentlemen?— these walls are solidly put together;" and here, through the mere phrenzy of bravado, I rapped heavily, with a cane which I held in my hand, upon that very portion of the brick-work behind which stood the corpse of the wife of my bosom.

But may God shield and deliver me from the fangs of the Arch-Fiend! No sooner had the reverberation of my blows sunk into silence, than I was answered by a voice from within the tomb!—by a cry, at first muffled and broken, like the sobbing of a child, and then quickly swelling into one long, loud, and continuous scream, utterly anomalous and inhuman—a howl—a wailing shriek, half of horror and half of triumph, such as might have arisen only out of hell, conjointly from the throats of the damned in their agony and of the demons that exult in the damnation.

Of my own thoughts it is folly to speak. Swooning, I staggered to the opposite wall. For one instant the party upon the stairs remained motionless, through extremity of terror and of awe. In the next, a dozen stout arms were toiling at the wall. It fell bodily. The corpse, already greatly decayed and clotted with gore, stood erect before the eyes of the spectators. Upon its head, with red extended mouth and solitary eye of fire, sat the hideous beast whose craft had seduced me into murder, and whose informing voice had consigned me to the hangman. I had walled the monster up within the tomb!

THE BLACK CAT'S MESSAGE

One never knows when the most sociable of cats may turn out to be a witch or "ha'nt," or to have evil concourse with the occult world. Elmira tells of an old couple with whom a big old yellow cat "took up." They were glad to have her, and treated her kindly. All went well until one day—

"The ole man was a wood-cutter. One evenin' as he was comin' home from his work, he saw a passel o' black cats out in the road. He looked to see what they was doin', an' theah was nine black cats totin' a little dead cat on a stretcher. He thought, 'Well, I never heard o' sich a thing as this: nine black cats totin' a little dead cat on a stretcher.'

"Jes then one o' them cats called out to the ole man an' says, 'Say, Mistuh, please tell Aunt Kan that Polly Grundy's daid.'

"The old man nevah answered 'em; he jes' walked on a little peahtah; but he thought, 'Um-m-m! If this ain't the beatin'est thing, them cats a-tellin' me to tell Aunt Kan that Polly Grundy's daid. Who is Aunt Kan, I wonder; an' who is Polly Grundy?'

"Well, he jes walked on, an' presen'y one of 'em hollered ag'in, an' say, 'Say, ole man, please tell Aunt Kan Polly Grundy's daid.'

"He jes walked on ag'in, gittin' a little faster all the time; an' presen'y all of 'em squall out: 'Hey there, old man, please suh, tell Aunt Kan Polly Grundy's daid.'

"Then the ole man he broke into a run, an' he nevah stopped till he got to his house. He thought he wouldn't tell his ole 'oman nothin' about it. But that night he was settin' befo' de fiah eatin' his suppah—ole folks lots o' times eats dey suppah befor' de fiah

—an' while his wife was a-settin' it foh 'im, he say. 'Well, Ole 'Oman, I guess I'll tell you some'n' dat I didn't think I would tell you.'

"When he say that, the ole yellow cat got up f'om de corner wheres she'uz a-laying', an' come ovah an' set down right by his chaiah, a-lookin' up at 'im.

"His ole 'oman say, 'Well, what is it, Ole Man? I knowed they'uz some'n' on yo' min' when you come in at dat do'.'

"He say, 'Well, when I 'uz comin' in from de woods dis evenin', walkin' down de road, right theah in de road I seen a whole passel o' black cats. When I went ovah an' looked theah was nine black cats a-totin' a little daid cat on a stretcher; an' them cats squall out to me three diffunt times an' tell me to tell Aunt Kan that Polly Grundy's daid.'

"When he say that, ole yellow cat jumped up an' say, 'Is she? B'God, I mus go to the buryin'!' An' out that do' she flew, an' she ain' nevah come back yit."

Southern Folk Tale, 19th Century

58

Jules Verne
1828-1905

FROM THE EARTH
TO THE MOON

A preparatory experiment, made on October 18th, gave the best results and excited the most promising hopes. Barbican, desirous to ascertain the effect of the concussion occurring at the instant of a projectile's departure, had a 32 inch mortar brought from Pensacola.

Into this harmless bombshell, which could be firmly closed by means of a screw fastened lid, they introduced first a large cat, then a very pretty squirrel belonging to Marston, who had made it quite a pet. The object of introducing the second animal was to ascertain how a living thing so slightly affected with vertigo as a squirrel, could endure the experimental trip.

The mortar was loaded with a charge of powder, the shell put in its place, and the piece fired off. The projectile shot up rapidly, describing its majestic parabola, reached a height of about a thousand feet, and then fell with a graceful curve into the midst of the waves. Without a moment's delay, a boat started for the spot; skilful divers plunging into the water and fastening cords to the ears of the shell, it was soon hauled aboard.

Ardan, Barbican, Marston, and McNicholl were all in the boat, and you can easily comprehend with what interest they watched the experiment. Scarcely was the lid opened, when out jumped the cat, a little scared and towzled, but as lively as ever, and evidently not a particle the worse for her äerial flight.

But no squirrel made his appearance. They waited for him. They looked for him. They shook the shell, and turned it upside down. No squirrel. There was no mincing the matter. The cat had eaten up her fellow traveller.

Cotton Mather
1663-1728

THE WONDERS OF
THE INVISIBLE WORLD

He said unto her, He believed she was a Witch. Whereat she being dissatisfied said, That some she-Devil would shortly fetch him away! Which words were heard by others, as well as himself. The Night following, as he lay in his Bed, there came in at the Window, the likeness of a Cat, which flew upon him, took fast hold of his Throat, lay on him a considerable while, and almost killed him. At length he remembered what Susanna Martin had threat'ned the Day before; and with much striving he cried out, Avoid, thou She-Devil! In the name of God the Father, the Son, and the Holy Ghost, Avoid! Whereupon it left him, leap'd on the Floor, and flew out at the Window.

George Bernard Shaw

1856-1950

CAESAR AND
CLEOPATRA

CLEOPATRA: ...Do you think that the black cat can have been my great-great-great-grandmother?
CAESAR: *(staring at her)* Your great-great-great-grandmother! Well, why not? Nothing would surprise me on this night of nights.
CLEOPATRA: I think it must have been. My great-grandmother's great-grandmother was a black kitten of the sacred white cat; and the river Nile made her his seventh wife. That is why my hair is so wavy.

Don Marquis

1878-1937

CHEERIO, MY DEARIO
(BY ARCHY THE COCKROACH)

well boss i met
mehitabel the cat
trying to dig a
frozen lamb chop
out of a snow
drift the other day

a heluva comedown
that is for me archy
she says a few
brief centuries
ago one of old
king
tut
ankh
amen s favourite
queens and today
the village scavenger
but wotthehell
archy wotthehell

I WAS CLEOPATRA ONCE
SHE SAID.

HERRIMAN

it s cheerio
my deario that
pulls a lady through

see here mehitabel
i said i thought
you told me that
it was cleopatra
you used to be
before you
transmigrated into
the carcase of a cat
where do you get
this tut
ankh
amen stuff
question mark

i was several
ladies my little
insect says she
being cleopatra was
only an incident
in my career
and i was always getting
the rough end of it
always being
misunderstood by some
strait laced
prune faced bunch
of prissy mouthed
sisters of uncharity

the things that
have been said
about me archy
exclamation point

and all simply
because i was a
live dame
the palaces i have
been kicked out of
in my time
exclamation point

but wotthehell
little archy wot
thehell
it s cheerio
my deario
that pulls a
lady through
exclamation point

framed archy always
framed that is the
story of all my lives
no chance for a dame
with the anvil chorus
if she shows a little
motion it seems to

me only yesterday
that the luxor local

number one of
the ladies axe
association got me in
dutch with king tut and
he slipped me the
sarcophagus always my
luck yesterday an empress
and today too
emaciated to interest
a vivisectionist but
toujours gai archy

toujours gai and always
a lady in spite of hell
and transmigration
once a queen
always a queen
archy
period

one of her
feet was frozen
but on the other three
she began to caper and
dance singing it s
cheerio my deario
that pulls a lady
through her morals may
have been mislaid somewhere
in the centuries boss but
i admire her spirit

archy

62

P.G.Wodehouse

1881-1975

THE STORY
OF WEBSTER

|C|ats are not dogs!"

There is only one place where you can hear good things like that thrown off quite casually in the general run of conversation, and that is the bar parlour of the *Angler's Rest*. It was there, as we sat grouped about the fire, that a thoughtful Pint of Bitter had made the statement just recorded.

Although the talk up to this point had been dealing with Einstein's Theory of Relativity, we readily adjusted our minds to cope with the new topic. Regular attendance at the nightly sessions over which Mr Mulliner presides with such unfailing dignity and geniality tends to produce mental nimbleness. In our little circle I have known an argument on the Final Destination of the Soul to change inside forty seconds into one concerning the best method of preserving the juiciness of bacon fat.

"Cats," proceeded the Pint of Bitter, "are selfish. A man waits on a cat hand and foot for weeks, humouring its lightest whim, and then it goes and leaves him flat because it has found a place down the road where the fish is more frequent."

"What I've got against cats," said a Lemon Sour, speaking feelingly, as one brooding on a private grievance, "is their unreliability. They lack candour and are not square shooters. You get your cat and you call him Thomas or George, as the case may be. So far, so good. Then one morning you wake up and find six kittens in the hat-box and you have to re-open the whole matter, approaching it from an entirely different angle."

"If you want to know what's the trouble with cats," said a red-faced man with glassy eyes, who had been rapping on the table for his fourth whisky, "they've got no tact. That's what's the trouble with them. I remember a friend of mine had a cat. Made quite a pet of that cat, he did. And what occurred? What was the outcome? One night he came home rather late and was feeling for the keyhole with his corkscrew; and, believe me or not, his cat selected that precise moment to jump on the back of his neck out of a tree. No tact."

Mr Mulliner shook his head.

"I grant you all this," he said, "but still, in my opinion, you have not got to the root of the matter. The real objection to the great majority of cats is their insufferable air of superiority. Cats, as a class, have never completely got over the snootiness caused by the fact that in Ancient Egypt they were worshipped as gods. This makes them too prone to set themselves up as critics and censors of the frail and erring human beings whose lot they share. They stare rebukingly. They view with concern. And on a sensitive man this often has the worst effects, inducing an inferiority complex of the gravest kind. It is odd that the conversation should have taken this turn," said Mr Mulliner, sipping his hot Scotch and lemon, "for I was thinking only this afternoon of the rather strange case of my cousin Edward's son, Lancelot."

"I knew a cat—" began a Small Bass.

My cousin Edward's son, Lancelot (said Mr Mulliner) was, at the time of which I speak, a comely youth of some twenty-five summers. Orphaned at an early age, he had been brought up in the home of his Uncle Theodore, the saintly Dean of Bolsover; and it was a great shock to that good man when Lancelot, on attaining his majority, wrote from London to inform him that he had taken a studio in Bott Street, Chelsea, and proposed to remain in the metropolis and become an artist.

The Dean's opinion of artists was low. As a prominent member of the Bolsover Watch Committee, it had recently been his distasteful duty to be present at a private showing of the super-super-film, *Palettes of Passion*; and he replied to his nephew's communication with a vibrant letter in which he emphasised the grievous pain it gave him to think that one of his flesh and blood should deliberately be embarking on a career which must inevitably lead sooner or later to the painting of Russian princesses lying on divans in the semi-nude with their arms round tame jaguars. He urged Lancelot to return and become a curate while there was yet time.

But Lancelot was firm. He deplored the rift between himself and a relative whom he had always respected; but he was dashed if he meant to go back to an environment where his individuality had been stifled and his soul confined in chains. And for four years there was silence between uncle and nephew.

During these years Lancelot had made progress in his chosen profession. At the time at which this story opens, his prospects seemed bright. He was painting the portrait of Brenda, only daughter of Mr and Mrs B. B. Carberry-Pirbright, of 11 Maxton Square, South Kensington, which meant thirty pounds in his sock on delivery. He had learned to cook eggs and bacon. He had practically mastered the ukulele. And, in addition, he was engaged to be married to a fearless young vers libre poetess of the name of Gladys Bingley, better known as The Sweet Singer of Garbidge Mews, Fulham—a charming girl who looked like a pen-wiper.

It seemed to Lancelot that life was very full and beautiful. He lived joyously in the present, giving no thought to the past.

But how true it is that the past is inextricably mixed up with the present and that we can never tell when it may spring some delayed bomb beneath our feet. One afternoon, as he sat making a few small alterations in the portrait of Brenda Carberry-Pirbright, his fiancée entered.

He had been expecting her to call, for today she was going off for a three weeks' holiday to the South of France, and she had promised to look in on her way to the station. He laid down his brush and gazed at her with a yearning affection, thinking for the thousandth time how he worshipped every spot of ink on her nose. Standing there in the doorway with her bobbed hair sticking out in every direction like a golliwog's, she made a picture that seemed to speak to his very depths.

"Hullo, Reptile!" he said lovingly.

"What ho, Worm!" said Gladys, maidenly devotion shining through the monocle which she wore in her left eye. "I can stay just half an hour."

"Oh, well, half an hour soon passes," said Lancelot. "What's that you've got there?"

"A letter, ass. What did you think it was?"

"Where did you get it?"

"I found the postman outside."

Lancelot took the envelope from her and examined it.

"Gosh!" he said.

"What's the matter?"

"It's from my Uncle Theodore."

"I didn't know you had an Uncle Theodore."

"Of course I have. I've had him for years."

"What's he writing to you about?"

"If you'll kindly keep quiet for two seconds, if you know how," said Lancelot, "I'll tell you."

And in a clear voice which, like that of all the Mulliners, however distant from the main branch, was beautifully modulated, he read as follows:

> The Deanery,
> Bolsover, Wilts.
>
> My dear Lancelot,
>
> As you have, no doubt, already learned from your *Church Times*, I have been offered and have accepted the vacant Bishopric of Bongo-Bongo, in West Africa. I sail immediately to take up my new duties, which I trust will be blessed.
>
> In these circumstances it becomes necessary for me to find a good home for my cat Webster. It is, alas, out of the question that he should accompany me, as the rigours of the climate and the lack of essential comforts might well sap a constitution which has never been robust.
>
> I am dispatching him, therefore, to your address, my dear boy, in a straw-lined hamper, in the full confidence that you will prove a kindly and conscientious host.
>
> With cordial good wishes,
> Your affectionate uncle,
> Theodore Bongo-Bongo

For some moments after he had finished reading this communication, a thoughtful silence prevailed in the studio.

"Of all the nerve!" she said. "I wouldn't do it."

"Why not?"

"What do you want with a cat?"

Lancelot reflected.

"It is true," he said, "that, given a free hand, I would prefer not to have my studio turned into a cattery or cat-bin. But consider the special circumstances. Relations between Uncle Theodore and self have for the last few years been a bit strained. In fact, you might say we have definitely parted brass-rags. It looks to me as if he were coming round. I should describe this letter as more or less what you might call an olive-branch. If I lush this cat up satisfactorily, shall I not be in a position later on to make a swift touch?"

"He is rich, this bean?" said Gladys, interested.

"Extremely."

"Then," said Gladys, "consider my objections withdrawn. A good stout cheque from a grateful cat-fancier would undoubtedly come in very handy. We might be able to get married this year."

"Exactly," said Lancelot. "A pretty loathsome prospect, of course; but still, as we've arranged to do it, the sooner we get it over, the better, what?"

"Absolutely."

"Then that's settled. I accept custody of cat."

"It's the only thing to do," said Gladys. "Meanwhile, can you lend me a comb? Have you such a thing in your bedroom?"

"What do you want with a comb?"

"I got some soup in my hair at lunch. I won't be a minute."

She hurried out, and Lancelot, taking up the letter again, found that he had omitted to read a continuation of it on the back page.

It was to the following effect:

PS. In establishing Webster in your home, I am actuated by another motive than the simple desire to see to it that my faithful friend and companion is adequately provided for.

From both a moral and an educative standpoint, I am convinced that Webster's society will prove of inestimable value to you. His advent, indeed, I venture to hope, will be a turning-point in your life. Thrown, as you must be, incessantly among loose and immoral Bohemians, you will find in this cat an example of upright conduct which cannot but act as an antidote to the poison cup of temptation which is, no doubt, hourly pressed to your lips.

PPS. Cream only at midday, and fish not more than three times a week.

He was reading these words for the second time, when the front-door bell rang and he found a man on the steps with a hamper. A discreet mew from within revealed its contents, and Lancelot, carrying it into the studio, cut the strings.

"Hi!" he bellowed, going to the door.

"What's up?" shrieked his betrothed from above.

"The cat's come."

"All right. I'll be down in a jiffy."

Lancelot returned to the studio.

"What ho, Webster!" he said cheerily. "How's the boy?"

The cat did not reply. It was sitting with bent head, performing that wash and brush up which a journey by rail renders so necessary.

In order to facilitate these toilet operations, it had raised its left leg and was holding it rigidly in the air. And there flashed into Lancelot's mind an old superstition handed on to him, for what it was worth, by one of the nurses of his infancy. If, this woman had said, you creep up to a cat when its leg is in the air, and give it a pull, then you make a wish and your wish comes true in thirty days.

It was a pretty fancy, and it seemed to Lancelot that the theory might as well be put to the test. He advanced warily, therefore, and was in the act of extending his fingers for the pull, when Webster, lowering the leg, turned and raised his eyes.

He looked at Lancelot. And suddenly with sickening force there came to Lancelot the realisation of the unpardonable liberty he had been about to take.

Until this moment, though the postscript to his uncle's letter should have warned him, Lancelot Mulliner had had no suspicion of what manner of cat this was that he had taken into his home. Now, for the first time, he saw him steadily and saw him whole.

Webster was very large and very black and very composed. He conveyed the impression of being a cat of deep reserves. Descendant of a long line of ecclesiastical ancestors who had conducted their decorous courtships beneath the shadow of cathedrals and on the back walls of bishops' palaces, he had that exquisite poise which one sees in high dignitaries of the Church. His eyes were clear and steady, and seemed to pierce to the very roots of the young man's soul, filling him with a sense of guilt.

Once, long ago, in his hot childhood, Lancelot, spending his summer holidays at the Deanery, had been so far carried away by ginger-beer and original sin as to plug a senior canon in the leg with his air-gun—only to discover, on turning, that a visiting archdeacon had been a spectator of the entire incident from his immediate rear. As he felt then, when meeting the archdeacon's eye, so did he feel now as Webster's gaze played silently upon him.

Webster, it is true, had not actually raised his eyebrows. But this, Lancelot felt, was simply because he hadn't any.

He backed, blushing.

"Sorry!" he muttered.

There was a pause. Webster continued his steady scrutiny. Lancelot edged towards the door.

"Er—excuse me—just a moment . . ." he mumbled. And, sidling from the room, he ran distractedly upstairs.

"I say," said Lancelot.

"Now what?" asked Gladys.

"Have you finished with the mirror?"

"Why?"

"Well, I—er—I thought," said Lancelot, "that I might as well have a shave."

The girl looked at him, astonished.

"Shave? Why, you shaved only the day before yesterday."

"I know. But, all the same . . . I mean to say, it seems only respectful. That cat, I mean."

"What about him?"

"Well, he seems to expect it, somehow. Nothing actually said, don't you know, but you could tell by his manner. I thought a quick shave and perhaps change into my blue serge suit—"

"He's probably thirsty. Why don't you give him some milk?"

"Could one, do you think?" said Lancelot doubtful. "I mean I hardly seem to know him well enough." He paused. "I say, old girl," he went on, with a touch of hesitation.

"Hullo?"

"I know you won't mind my mentioning it, but you've got a few spots of ink on your nose."

"Of course I have. I always have spots of ink on my nose."

"Well . . . you don't think . . . a quick scrub with a bit of pumice-stone . . . I mean to say, you know how important first impressions are . . ."

The girl stared.

"Lancelot Mulliner," she said, "if you think I'm going to skin my nose to the bone just to please a mangy cat—"

"Sh!" cried Lancelot, in agony.

"Here, let me go down and look at him," said Gladys petulantly.

As they re-entered the studio, Webster was gazing with an air of quiet distaste at an illustration from *La Vie Parisienne* which adorned one of the walls. Lancelot tore it down hastily.

Gladys looked at Webster in an unfriendly way.

"So that's the blighter!"

"Sh!"

"If you want to know what I think," said Gladys, "that cat's been living too high. Doing himself a dashed sight too well. You'd better cut his rations down a bit."

In substance, her criticism was not unjustified. Certainly, there was about Webster more than a suspicion of embonpoint. He had that air of portly well-being which we associate with those who dwell in cathedral closes. But Lancelot winced uncomfortably. He had so hoped that Gladys would make a good impression, and here she was, starting right off by saying the tactless thing.

He longed to explain to Webster that it was only her way; that in the Bohemian circles of which she was such an ornament genial chaff of a personal order was accepted and, indeed, relished. But it was too late. The mischief had been done. Webster turned in a pointed manner and withdrew silently behind the chesterfield.

Gladys, all unconscious, was making preparations for departure.

"Well, bung-ho," she said lightly. "See you in three weeks. I suppose you and that cat'll both be out on the tiles the moment my back's turned."

"Please! Please!" moaned Lancelot. "Please!"

He had caught sight of the tip of a black tail protruding from behind the chesterfield. It was twitching slightly, and Lancelot could read it like a book. With a sickening sense of dismay, he knew that Webster had formed a snap judgment of his fiancée and condemned her as frivolous and unworthy.

It was some ten days later than Bernard Worple,

the neo-Vorticist sculptor, lunching at the Puce Ptarmigan, ran into Rodney Scollop, the powerful young surrealist. And after talking for a while of their art:

"What's all this I hear about Lancelot Mulliner?" asked Worple. "There's a wild story going about that he was seen shaved in the middle of the week. Nothing in it, I suppose?"

Scollop looked grave. He had been on the point of mentioning Lancelot himself, for he loved the lad and was deeply exercised about him.

"It is perfectly true," he said.

"It sounds incredible."

Scollop leaned forward. His fine face was troubled.

"Shall I tell you something, Worple?"

"What?"

"I know for an absolute fact," said Scollop, "that Lancelot Mulliner now shaves every morning."

Worple pushed aside the spaghetti which he was wreathing about him and through the gap stared at his companion.

"Every morning?"

"Every single morning. I looked in on him myself the other day, and there he was, neatly dressed in blue serge and shaved to the core. And, what is more, I got the distinct impression that he had used talcum powder afterwards."

"You don't mean that!"

"I do. And shall I tell you something else? There was a book lying open on the table. He tried to hide it, but he wasn't quick enough. It was one of those etiquette books!"

"An etiquette book!"

"*Polite Behaviour*, by Constance, Lady Bodbank."

Worple unwound a stray tendril of spaghetti from about his left ear. He was deeply agitated. Like Scollop, he loved Lancelot.

"He'll be dressing for dinner next!" he exclaimed.

"I have every reason to believe," said Scollop gravely, "that he does dress for dinner. At any rate, a man closely resembling him was seen furtively buying three stiff collars and a black tie at Hope Brothers in the King's Road last Tuesday."

Worple pushed his chair back, and rose. His manner was determined.

"Scollop," he said, "we are friends of Mulliner's, you and I. It is evident from what you tell me that subversive influences are at work and that never has he needed our friendship more. Shall we not go round and see him immediately?"

"It was what I was about to suggest myself," said Rodney Scollop.

Twenty minutes later they were in Lancelot's studio, and with a significant glance Scollop drew his companion's notice to their host's appearance. Lancelot Mulliner was neatly, even foppishly, dressed in blue serge with creases down the trouser-legs, and his chin, Worple saw with a pang, gleamed smoothly in the afternoon light.

At the sight of his friends' cigars, Lancelot exhibited unmistakable concern.

"You don't mind throwing those away, I'm sure," he said pleadingly.

Rodney Scollop drew himself up a little haughtily.

"And since when," he asked, "have the best fourpenny cigars in Chelsea not been good enough for you?"

Lancelot hastened to soothe him.

"It isn't me," he exclaimed. "It's Webster. My cat. I happen to know he objects to tobacco smoke. I had to give up my pipe in deference to his views."

Bernard Worple snorted.

"Are you trying to tell us," he sneered, "that Lancelot Mulliner allows himself to be dictated to by a blasted cat?"

"Hush!" cried Lancelot, trembling. "If you knew how he disapproves of strong language!"

"Where is this cat?" asked Rodney Scollop. "Is that the animal?" he said, pointing out of the window to where, in the yard, a tough-looking Tom with tattered ears stood mewing in a hardboiled way out of the corner of its mouth.

"Good heavens, no!" said Lancelot. "That is an alley cat which comes around here from time to time to lunch at the dustbin. Webster is quite different. Webster has a natural dignity and repose of manner. Webster is a cat who prides himself on always being well turned out and whose high principles and lofty ideals shine from his eyes like beacon fires . . ." And then suddenly, with an abrupt change of manner, Lancelot broke down and in a low voice added, "Curse him! Curse him! Curse him! Curse him!"

Worple looked at Scollop. Scollop looked at Worple.

"Come, old man," said Scollop, laying a gentle hand on Lancelot's bowed shoulder. "We are your friends. Confide in us."

"Tell us all," said Worple. "What's the matter?"

Lancelot uttered a bitter, mirthless laugh.

"You want to know what's the matter? Listen, then. I'm cat-pecked!"

"Cat-pecked?"

"You've heard of men being hen-pecked, haven't you?" said Lancelot with a touch of irritation. "Well, I'm cat-pecked."

And in broken accents he told his story. He sketched the history of his association with Webster from the latter's first entry into the studio. Confident now that the animal was not within earshot, he unbosomed himself without reserve.

"It's something in the beast's eye," he said in a shaking voice. "Something hypnotic. He casts a spell upon me. He gazes at me and disapproves. Little by little, bit by bit, I am degenerating under his influence from a wholesome, self-respecting artist into . . . well, I don't know what you call it. Suffice it to say that I have given up smoking, that I have ceased to wear carpet slippers and go about without a collar, that I never dream of sitting down to my frugal evening meal without dressing, and"—he choked—"I have sold my ukulele."

"Not that!" said Worple, paling.

"Yes," said Lancelot. "I felt he considered it frivolous."

There was a long silence.

"Mulliner," said Scollop, "this is more serious that I had supposed. We must brood upon your case."

"It may be possible," said Worple, "to find a way out."

Lancelot shook his head hopelessly.

"There is no way out. I have explored every avenue. The only thing that could possibly free me from this intolerable bondage would be if once—just once—I could catch that cat unbending. If once—merely once—it would lapse in my presence from its austere dignity for but a single instant, I feel that the spell would be broken. But what hope is there of that?" cried Lancelot passionately. "You were pointing just now to that alley cat in the yard. There stands one who has strained every nerve and spared no effort to break down Webster's inhuman self-control. I have heard that animal say things to him which you would think no cat with red blood in its veins would suffer for an instant. And Webster merely looks at him like a Suffragan Bishop eyeing an erring choirboy and turns his head and falls into a refreshing sleep."

He broke off with a dry sob. Worple, always an optimist, attempted in his kindly way to minimise the tragedy.

"Ah, well," he said. "It's bad, of course, but still, I suppose there is no actual harm in shaving and dressing for dinner and so on. Many great artists . . . Whistler, for example—"

"Wait!" cried Lancelot. "You have not heard the worst."

He rose feverishly, and, going to the easel, disclosed the portrait of Brenda Carberry-Pirbright.

"Take a look at that," he said, "and tell me what you think of her."

His two friends surveyed the face before them in silence. Miss Carberry-Pirbright was a young woman of prim and glacial aspect. One sought in vain for her reasons for wanting to have her portrait painted. It would be a most unpleasant thing to have about any house.

Scollop broke the silence.

"Friend of yours?"

"I can't stand the sight of her," said Lancelot vehemently.

"Then," said Scollop, "I may speak frankly. I think she's a pill."

"A blister," said Worple.

"A boil and a disease," said Scollop, summing up.

Lancelot laughed hackingly.

"You have described her to a nicety. She stands for everything most alien to my artist soul. She gives me a pain in the neck. I'm going to marry her."

"What!" cried Scollop.

"But you're going to marry Gladys Bingley," said Worple.

"Webster thinks not," said Lancelot bitterly. "At their first meeting he weighed Gladys in the balance and found her wanting. And the moment he saw Brenda Carberry-Pirbright he stuck his tail up at right angles, uttered a cordial gargle, and rubbed his head against her leg. Then turning, he looked at me. I could read that glance. I knew what was in his mind. From that moment he has been doing everything in his power to arrange the match."

"But, Mulliner," said Worple, always eager to pointed out the bright side, "why should this girl want to marry a wretched, scrubby, hard-up footler like you? Have courage, Mulliner. It is simply a question of time before you repel and sicken her."

Lancelot shook his head.

"No," he said. "You speak like a true friend, Worple, but you do not understand. Old Ma Carberry-Pirbright, this exhibit's mother, who chaperons her at the sittings, discovered at an early date my relationship to my Uncle Theodore, who, as you know, has got it in gobs. She knows well enough that some day I shall be a rich man. She used to know my Uncle Theodore when he was Vicar of St Botolph's in Knightsbridge, and from the very first she assumed towards me the repellent chumminess of an old family friend. She was always trying to lure me to her At Homes, her Sunday luncheons, her little dinners. Once she actually suggested that I should escort her and her beastly daughter to the Royal Academy."

He laughed bitterly. The mordant witticisms of Lancelot Mulliner at the expense of the Royal Academy were quoted from Tite Street in the south to Holland Park in the north and eastward as far as Bloomsbury.

"To all these overtures," resumed Lancelot, "I remained firmly unresponsive. My attitude was from the start one of frigid aloofness. I did not actually say in so many words that I would rather be dead in a ditch than at one of her At Homes, but my manner indicated it. And I was just beginning to think I had choked her off when in crashed Webster and upset everything. Do you know how many times I have been to that infernal house in the last week? Five. Webster seemed to wish it. I tell you, I am a lost man."

He buried his face in his hands. Scollop touched Worple on the arm, and together the two men stole silently out.

"Bad!" said Worple.

"Very bad," said Scollop.

"It seems incredible."

"Oh, no. Cases of this kind are, alas, by no means uncommon among those who, like Mulliner, possess to a marked degree the highly-strung, ultrasensitive artistic temperament. A friend of mine, a rhythmical interior decorator, once rashly consented to put his aunt's parrot up at his studio while she was away visiting friends in the north of England. She was a woman of strong evangelical views, which the bird had imbibed from her. It had a way of putting its head on one side, making a noise like someone drawing a cork from a bottle, and asking my friend if he was saved. To cut a long story short, I happened to call on him a month later and he had installed a harmonium in his studio and was singing hymns, ancient and modern, in a rich tenor, while the parrot, standing on one leg on its perch, took the bass. A very sad affair. We were all much upset about it."

Worple shuddered.

"You appal me, Scollop! Is there nothing we can do?"

Rodney Scollop considered for a moment.

"We might wire Gladys Bingley to come home at once. She might possibly reason with the unhappy man. A woman's gentle influence . . . Yes, we could do that. Look in at the post office on your way home and send Gladys a telegram. I'll owe you for my half of it."

In the studio they had left, Lancelot Mulliner was staring dumbly at a black shape which had just entered the room. He had the appearance of a man with his back to the wall.

"No!" he was crying. "No! I'm dashed if I do!"

Webster continued to look at him.

"Why should I?" demanded Lancelot weakly.

Webster's gaze did not flicker.

"Oh, all right," said Lancelot sullenly.

He passed from the room with leaden feet, and, proceeding upstairs, changed into morning clothes and a top hat. Then, with a gardenia in his buttonhole, he made his way to 11 Maxton Square, where Mrs Carberry-Pirbright was giving one of her intimate little teas ("just a few friends") to meet Clara Throckmorton Stooge, authoress of *A Strong Man's Kiss*.

Gladys Bingley was lunching at her hotel in Antibes when Worple's telegram arrived. It occasioned her the gravest concern.

Exactly what it was all about she was unable to gather, for emotion had made Bernard Worple rather incoherent. There were moments, reading it, when she fancied that Lancelot had met with a serious accident; others when the solution seemed to be that he had sprained his brain to such an extent that rival lunatic asylums were competing eagerly for his custom; others, again, when Worple appeared to be suggesting that he had gone into partnership with his cat to start a harem. But one fact emerged clearly. Her loved one was in serious trouble of some kind, and his best friends were agreed that only her immediate return could save him.

Gladys did not hesitate. Within half an hour of the receipt of the telegram she had packed her trunk, removed a piece of asparagus from her right eyebrow, and was negotiating for accommodation on the first train going north.

Arriving in London, her first impulse was to go straight to Lancelot. But a natural feminine curiosity urged her, before doing so, to call upon Bernard Worple and have light thrown on some of the more abstruse passages in the telegram.

Worple, in his capacity of author, may have tended towards obscurity, but, when confining himself to the spoken word, he told a plain story well and clearly. Five minutes of his society enabled Gladys to obtain a firm grasp on the salient facts, and there appeared on her face that grim, tight-lipped expression which is seen only on the faces of fiancées who have come back from a short holiday

to discover that their dear one has been straying in their absence from the straight and narrow path.

"Brenda Carberry-Pirbright, eh?" said Gladys, with ominous calm. "I'll give him Brenda Carberry-Pirbright! My gosh, if one can't go off to Antibes for the merest breather without having one's betrothed getting it up his nose and starting to act like a Mormon Elder, it begins to look a pretty tough world for a girl."

"I blame the cat," he said. "Lancelot, to my mind, is more sinned against than sinning. I consider him to be acting under undue influence or duress."

"How like a man!" said Gladys. "Shoving it all off on to an innocent cat!"

"Lancelot says it has a sort of something in its eye."

"Well, when I meet Lancelot," said Gladys, "he'll find that I have a sort of something in my eye."

She went out, breathing flame quietly through her nostrils. Worple, saddened, heaved a sigh and resumed his neo-Vorticist sculpting.

It was some five minutes later that Gladys, passing through Maxton Square on her way to Bott Street, stopped suddenly in her tracks. The sight she had seen was enough to make any fiancée do so.

Along the pavement leading to No. 11 two figures were advancing. Or three, if you counted a morose-looking dog of a semi-dachshund nature which preceded them, attached to a leash. One of the figures was that of Lancelot Mulliner, natty in grey herring-bone tweed and a new Homburg hat. It was he who held the leash. The other Gladys recognized from the portrait which she had seen on Lancelot's easel as that modern Du Barry, that notorious wrecker of homes and breaker-up of love-nests, Brenda Carberry-Pirbright.

The next moment they had mounted the steps of No. 11, and had gone in to tea, possibly with a little music.

It was perhaps an hour and a half later that Lancelot, having wrenched himself with difficulty from the lair of the Philistines, sped homeward in a swift taxi. As always after an extended tete-à-tete with Miss Carberry-Pirbright, he felt dazed and bewildered, as if he had been swimming in a sea of glue and had swallowed a good deal of it. All he could think of clearly was that he wanted a drink and that the materials for that drink were in the cupboard behind the chesterfield in his studio.

He paid the cab and charged in with his tongue rattling dryly against his front teeth. And there before him was Gladys Bingley, whom he had supposed far, far away.

"You!" exclaimed Lancelot.

"Yes, me!" said Gladys.

Her long vigil had not helped to restore the girl's equanimity. Since arriving at the studio she had had leisure to tap her foot three thousand, one hundred and forty-two times on the carpet, and the number of bitter smiles which had flitted across her face was nine hundred and eleven. She was about ready for the battle of the century.

She rose and faced him all the woman in her flashing from her eyes.

"Well, you Casanova!" she said.

"You who?" said Lancelot.

"Don't say 'Yoo-hoo!' to me!" cried Gladys. "Keep that for your Brenda Carberry-Pirbright. Yes, I know all about it, Lancelot Don Juan Henry the Eighth Mulliner! I saw you with her just now. I hear that you and she are inseparable. Bernard Worple says you said you were going to marry her."

"You mustn't believe everything a neo-Vorticist sculptor tells you," quavered Lancelot.

"I'll bet you're going back to dinner there tonight," said Gladys.

She had spoken at a venture, basing the charge purely on a possessive cock of the head which she had noticed in Brenda Carberry-Pirbright at their recent encounter. There, she had said to herself at the time, had gone a girl who was about to invite— or had just invited—Lancelot Mulliner to dine quietly and take her to the pictures afterwards. But the shot went home. Lancelot hung his head.

"There was some talk of it," he admitted.

"Ah!" exclaimed Gladys.

Lancelot's eyes were haggard.

"I don't want to go," he pleaded. "Honestly, I don't. But Webster insists."

"Webster!"

"Yes, Webster. If I attempt to evade the appointment, he will sit in front of me and look at me."

"Tchah!"

"Well, he will. Ask him for yourself."

Gladys tapped her foot six times in rapid succession on the carpet, bringing the total to three thousand, one hundred and forty-eight. Her manner had changed and was now dangerously calm.

"Lancelot Mulliner," she said, "you have your choice. Me, on the one hand, Brenda Carberry-Pirbright on the other. I offer you a home where you will be able to smoke in bed, spill the ashes on the floor, wear pyjamas and carpet slippers all day and shave only on Sunday mornings. From her,

what have you to hope? A house in South Kensington—possibly the Brompton Road—probably with her mother living with you. A life that will be one long round of stiff collars and tight shoes, of morning coats and top hats."

Lancelot quivered, but she went on remorselessly.

"You will be at home on alternate Thursdays, and will be expected to hand the cucumber sandwiches. Every day you will air the dog, till you become a confirmed dog-airer. You will dine out in Bayswater and go for the summer to Bournemouth or Dinard. Choose well, Lancelot Mulliner! I will leave you to think it over. But one last word. If by seven-thirty on the dot you have not presented yourself at 6a Garbidge Mews ready to take me out to dinner at the Ham and Beef, I shall know what to think and shall act accordingly."

And brushing the cigarette ashes from her chin, the girl strode haughtily from the room.

"Gladys!" cried Lancelot.

But she had gone.

For some minutes Lancelot Mulliner remained where he was, stunned. Then, insistently, there came to him the recollection that he had not had that drink. He rushed to the cupboard and produced the bottle. He uncorked it, and was pouring out a lavish stream, when a movement on the floor below him attracted his attention.

Webster was standing there, looking up at him. And in his eyes was that familiar expression of quiet rebuke.

"Scarcely what I have been accustomed to at the Deanery," he seemed to be saying.

Lancelot stood paralysed. The feeling of being bound hand and foot, of being caught in a snare from which there was no escape, had become more poignant than ever. The bottle fell from his nerveless fingers and rolled across the floor, spilling its contents in an amber river, but he was too heavy in spirit to notice it. With a gesture such as Job might have made on discovering a new boil, he crossed to the window and stood looking moodily out.

Then, turning with a sigh, he looked at Webster again—and, looking, stood spell-bound.

The spectacle which he beheld was of a kind to stun a stronger man than Lancelot Mulliner. At first, he shrank from believing his eyes. Then, slowly, came the realisation that what he saw was no mere figment of a disordered imagination. This unbelievable thing was actually happening.

Webster sat crouched upon the floor beside the widening pool of whisky. But it was not horror and disgust that had caused him to crouch. He was crouched because, crouching, he could get nearer to the stuff and obtain crisper action. His tongue was moving in and out like a piston.

And then abruptly, for one fleeting instant, he stopped lapping and glanced up at Lancelot, and across his face there flitted a quick smile—so genial, so intimate, so full of jovial camaraderie, that the young man found himself automatically smiling back, and not only smiling but winking. And in answer to that wink Webster winked too—a whole-hearted, roguish wink that said as plainly as if he had spoken the words:

"How long has this been going on?"

Then with a slight hiccough he turned back to the task of getting his drink before it soaked into the floor.

Into the murky soul of Lancelot Mulliner there poured a sudden flood of sunshine. It was as if a great burden had been lifted from his shoulders. The intolerable obsession of the last two weeks had ceased to oppress him, and he felt a free man. At the eleventh hour the reprieve had come. Webster, that seeming pillar of austere virtue, was one of the boys, after all. Never again would Lancelot quail beneath his eye. He had the goods on him.

Webster, like the stag at eve, had now drunk his fill. He had left the pool of alcohol and was walking round in slow, meditative circles. From time to time he mewed tentatively, as if he were trying to say "British Constitution". His failure to articulate the syllables appeared to tickle him, for at the end of each attempt he would utter a slow, amused chuckle. It was about this moment that he suddenly broke into a rhythmic dance, not unlike the old Saraband.

It was an interesting spectacle, and at any other time Lancelot would have watched it raptly. But now he was busy at his desk, writing a brief note to Mrs Carberry-Pirbright, the burden of which was that if she thought he was coming within a mile of her foul house that night or any other night she had vastly underrated the dodging powers of Lancelot Mulliner.

And what of Webster? The Demon Rum now had him in an iron grip. A lifetime of abstinence had rendered him a ready victim to the fatal fluid. He had now reached the stage when geniality gives way to belligerence. The rather foolish smile had gone from his face, and in its stead there lowered a fighting frown. For a few moments he stood on his hind legs, looking about him for a suitable adversary: then, losing all vestiges of self-control, he ran five times round the room at a high rate of speed and,

falling foul of a small footstool, attacked it with the utmost ferocity, sparing neither tooth nor claw.

But Lancelot did not see him. Lancelot was not there. Lancelot was out in Bott Street, hailing a cab.

"6a Garbidge Mews, Fulham," said Lancelot to the driver.

Ambrose Bierce
1842-1914

FABLES

A cat was looking at a King, as permitted by the proverb.

" 'Well,' said the Monarch, observing her inspection of the royal person, 'how do you like me?'

" 'I can imagine a King,' said the Cat, 'whom I should like better.'

" 'For example?'

" 'The King of the Mice.'

"The sovereign was so pleased with the wit of the reply that he gave her permission to scratch his Prime Minister's eyes out."

"A Cat fell in love with a handsome Young Man, and entreated Venus to change her into a woman.

" 'I should think,' said Venus, 'you might make so trifling a change without bothering me. However, be a woman.'

"Afterward, wishing to see if the change were complete, Venus caused a mouse to approach, whereupon the woman shrieked and made such a show of herself that the Young Man would not marry her."

"Hearing that the Birds in an aviary were ill, a Cat went to them and said that he was a physician, and would cure them if they would let him in.

" 'To what school of medicine do you belong?' asked the Birds.

" 'I am a Miaulopathist,' said the Cat.

" 'Did you ever practice Gohomœopathy?' the Birds inquired, winking faintly.

"The Cat took the hint and his leave."

A harmless necessary cat.   *Shakespeare*

Eugène Mihaesco

William Carlos Williams

1883-1963

POEM

As the cat
climbed over
the top of

the jamcloset
first the right
forefoot

carefully
then the hind
stepped down

into the pit of
the empty
flowerpot.

PUSS-PUSS

—Oh, Auntie, isn't he a beauty! And is he a
  gentleman or a lady?
—Neither, my dear! I had him fixed. It saves him
  from so many undesirable associations.

D. H. Lawrence

THE FORMIDABLE
"GIPSY"

His extraordinary size, his daring, and his utter
lack of sympathy soon made him the leader—and,
at the same time, the terror—of all the loose-lived
cats in a wide neighbourhood. He contracted no
friendships and had no confidents. He seldom slept
in the same place twice in succession, and though
he was wanted by the police, he was not found. In
appearance he did not lack distinction of an ominous sort; the slow, rhythmic, perfectly controlled
mechanism of his tail, as he impressively walked
abroad, was incomparably sinister.

Booth Tarkington

Don't offer me your cat. If my cat does not come
back I don't mean to have a cat for some time. Jones
has a real love of a cat, and when my mice get bad I
will fetch it down for a day or two.

Samuel Butler

74

Ernest Hemingway

1899-1961

CAT IN
THE RAIN

There were only two Americans stopping at the hotel. They did not know any of the people they passed on the stairs on their way to and from their room. Their room was on the second floor facing the sea. It also faced the public garden and the war monument. There were big palms and green benches in the public garden. In the good weather there was always an artist with his easel. Artists liked the way the palms grew and the bright colors of the hotels facing the gardens and the sea. Italians came from a long way off to look up at the war monument. It was made of bronze and glistened in the rain. It was raining. The rain dripped from the palm trees. Water stood in pools on the gravel paths. The sea broke in a long line in the rain and slipped back down the beach to come up and break again in a long line in the rain. The motor cars were gone from the square by the war monument. Across the square in the doorway of the café a waiter stood looking out at the empty square.

The American wife stood at the window looking out. Outside right under their window a cat was crouched under one of the dripping green tables. The cat was trying to make herself so compact that she would not be dripped on.

"I'm going down and get that kitty," the American wife said.

"I'll do it," her husband offered from the bed.

"No, I'll get it. The poor kitty out trying to keep dry under a table."

The husband went on reading, lying propped up with the two pillows at the foot of the bed.

"Don't get wet," he said.

The wife went downstairs and the hotel owner stood up and bowed to her as she passed the office. His desk was at the far end of the office. He was an old man and very tall.

"Il piove," the wife said. She liked the hotel-keeper.

"Si, si, Signora, brutto tempo. It's very bad weather."

He stood behind his desk in the far end of the dim room. The wife liked him. She liked the deadly serious way he received any complaints. She liked his dignity. She liked the way he wanted to serve her. She liked the way he felt about being a hotel-keeper. She liked his old, heavy face and big hands.

Liking him she opened the door and looked out. It was raining harder. A man in a rubber cape was crossing the empty square to the café. The cat would be around to the right. Perhaps she could go along under the eaves. As she stood in the doorway an umbrella opened behind her. It was the maid who looked after their room.

"You must not get wet," she smiled, speaking Italian. Of course, the hotel-keeper had sent her.

With the maid holding the umbrella over her, she walked along the gravel path until she was under their window. The table was there, washed bright green in the rain, but the cat was gone. She was suddenly disappointed. The maid looked up at her.

"Ha perduto qualque cosa, Signora?"

"There was a cat," said the American girl.

"A cat?"

"Si, el gatto."

"A cat?" the maid laughed. "A cat in the rain?"

"Yes," she said, "under the table." Then, "Oh, I wanted it so much. I wanted a kitty."

When she talked English the maid's face tightened.

"Come, Signora," she said. "We must get back inside. You will be wet."

"I suppose so," said the American girl.

They went back along the gravel path and passed in the door. The maid stayed outside to close the umbrella. As the American girl passed the office, the padrone bowed from his desk. Something felt very small and tight inside the girl. The padrone made her feel very small and at the same time really important. She had a momentary feeling of being of supreme importance. She went on up the stairs. She opened the door of the room. George was on the bed, reading.

"Did you get the cat?" he asked, putting the book down.

"It was gone."

"Wonder where it went to," he said, resting his eyes from reading.

She sat down on the bed.

"I wanted it so much," she said. "I don't know why I wanted it so much. I wanted that poor kitty. It isn't any fun to be a poor kitty out in the rain."

George was reading again.

She went over and sat in front of the mirror of the dressing table looking at herself with the hand glass. She studied her profile, first one side and then the other. Then she studied the back of her head and her neck.

"Don't you think it would be a good idea if I let my hair grow out?" she asked, looking at her profile again.

George looked up and saw the back of her neck, clipped close like a boy's.

"I like it the way it is."

"I get so tired of it," she said. "I get so tired of looking like a boy."

George shifted his position in the bed. He hadn't looked away from her since she started to speak.

"You look pretty darn nice," he said.

She laid the mirror down on the dresser and went over to the window and looked out. It was getting dark.

"I want to pull my hair back tight and smooth and make a big knot at the back that I can feel," she said. "I want to have a kitty to sit on my lap and purr when I stroke her."

" Yeah?" George said from the bed.

78

"And I want to eat at a table with my own silver and I want candles. And I want it to be spring and I want to brush my hair out in front of a mirror and I want a kitty and I want some new clothes."

"Oh, shut up and get something to read," George said. He was reading again.

His wife was looking out of the window. It was quite dark now and still raining in the palm trees.

"Anyway, I want a cat," she said, "I want a cat. I want a cat now. If I can't have long hair or any fun, I can have a cat."

George was not listening. He was reading his book. His wife looked out of the window where the light had come on in the square.

Someone knocked at the door.

"Avanti," George said. He looked up from his book.

In the doorway stood the maid. She held a big tortoise-shell cat pressed tight against her and swung down against her body.

"Excuse me," she said, "the padrone asked me to bring this for the Signora."

Colette
1873-1954

THE CAT
(EXCERPT)

One evening in July, when the two of them were waiting for Alain's return, Camille and the cat were resting on the same parapet; the cat crouched on all four paws, Camille leaning on her folded arms. Camille did not like this balcony-terrace, reserved for the cat and shut in by two cement partitions which cut off both the wind and all communication with the balcony on the prow.

They exchanged a glance of sheer mutual investigation and Camille did not say a word to Saha. Propped on her elbows, she leant over as if to count the storeys by the orange awnings that flapped from top to bottom of the dizzy façade, she brushed against the cat who got up to make room for her, stretched, and lay down a little further off.

When Camille was alone, she looked very much like the little girl who did not want to say 'how d'you do?' Her face returned to childhood because it wore that expression of inhuman innocence, of angelic hardness which ennobles children's faces. Her gaze wandered over Paris, over the sky from which the light drained a little earlier each day, with an impartial severity which possibly condemned nothing. She yawned nervously, stood upright and took a few absent-minded steps. Then she leant over again, forcing the cat to jump down. Saha stalked away with dignity and would have preferred to go back into the room. But the door in the hypotenuse had been shut and Saha patiently sat down. The next moment she had to get out of Camille's way for she was pacing from one partition to the other with long, jerky strides. The cat jumped back on to the parapet. As if in play, Camille dislodged her as she leant on her elbows and once again Saha took refuge against the closed door.

Motionless, her eyes far away, Camille stood with her back to her. Nevertheless the cat was looking at Camille's back and her breath came faster. She got up, turned two or three times on her own axis and looked questioningly at the closed door. Camille had not moved. Saha inflated her nostrils and showed a distress which was almost like nausea. A long, desolate mew escaped from her, the wretched reply to a silent, imminent threat. Camille faced round abruptly.

She was a trifle pale; that is to say, her rouge stood out in two oval moons on her cheeks. She affected an air of absent-mindedness as she would if a human eye had been staring at her. She even began to sing under her breath and resumed her pacing from one partition to the other, pacing to the rhythm of her song, but her voice failed her. She forced the cat, whom her foot was about to kick, to regain her narrow observation post with one bound, then to flatten herself against the door.

Saha had regained her self-control and would have died rather than utter a second cry. Tracking the cat down, without appearing to see her, Camille paced to and fro in silence. Saha did not jump on the parapet till Camille's feet were right on top of her and she only leapt down again on to the floor of the balcony to avoid the outstretched arm which would have hurled her from the height of the nine storeys.

She fled methodically and jumped carefully, keeping her eyes fixed on her adversary and condescending neither to fury nor to supplication. The most violent emotion of all, the terror of dying, soaked the sensitive soles of her paws with sweat so that they left flower-like prints on the stucco balcony.

Camille seemed the first to weaken and to lose her criminal strength. She made the mistake of noticing that the sun was going down, gave a glance at her wrist watch, and was aware of the clink of glasses inside. A moment or two more and her resolution would have deserted her as sleep deserts the somnambulist, leaving her guiltless and exhausted. Saha felt her enemy's firmness waver, hesitated on the parapet and Camille, stretching out both arms, pushed her into space.

She had time to hear the grating of claws on the rough-cast wall, to see Saha's blue body, twisted into an S, clutching the air with the force of a rising trout; then she shrank away, with her back to the wall.

She felt no temptation to look down into the little kitchen garden edged with new rubble. Back in the room, she put her hands over her ears, withdrew them and shook her head as if she could hear the hum of a mosquito. Then she sat down and nearly fell asleep. But the oncoming night brought her to her feet again. She drove away the twilight by lighting up glass bricks, luminous tubes and blinding mushrooms of lamps. She also lit up the long chromium eye which poured the opaline beam of its glance across the bed.

She walked about with supple movements, handling objects with light, adroit, dreaming hands.

It's as if I'd got thinner," she said out loud.

She changed her clothes and dressed herself in white.

"My fly in the milk," she said, imitating Alain's voice. Her cheeks regained their colour at a sudden, sensual memory which brought her back to reality and she waited for Alain's arrival.

She bent her head in the direction of the buzzing lift and shivered at every noise; those dull knockings, those metallic clangs, those sounds as of a boat grinding at anchor, those muffled bursts of music which echo the discordant life of a new block of flats. But she was not surprised when the hollow tinkle of the bell in the hall replaced the fumbling of a key in the lock. She ran and opened the door herself.

"Shut the door," Alain ordered. "I must see first of all whether she hasn't hurt herself. Come and hold the lamp for me."

He carried Saha alive in his arms. He went straight to the bedroom, pushed aside the things on the invisible dressing-table and gently put the cat on the slab of glass. She held herself upright and firm on her paws but her deep-set eyes wandered all about her as they would have done in a strange house.

"Saha!" called Alain in a whisper. "If there's nothing the matter with her, it's a miracle. Saha!"

She raised her head, as if to reassure her friend, and leant her cheek against his hand.

"Walk a little, Saha. Look, she's walking! Good Lord! Falling six storeys! It was the awning of the chap on the second floor that broke the fall. From there she bounced off on to the concierges' little lawn—the concierge saw her pass in the air. He said: 'I thought it was an umbrella falling' What's she got on her ear? No, it's some white off the wall. Wait till I listen to her heart."

He laid the cat on her side and listened to the beating ribs, the tiny disordered mechanism. With his fair hair spread out and his eyes closed, he seemed to be sleeping on Saha's flank and to wake with a sigh only to see Camille standing there silent and apart, watching the close-knit group they made.

"Can you believe it? There's nothing wrong. At least I can't find anything wrong with her except a terribly agitated heart. But a cat's heart is usually agitated. But however could it have happened! I'm asking you as if you could possibly know, my poor pet! She fell from this side," he said, looking at the open french window. "Jump down on the ground, Saha, if you can."

After hesitating, she jumped but lay down again on the carpet. She was breathing fast and went on looking all round the room with the same uncertain look.

"I think I'll 'phone Chéron. Still, look, she's washing herself. She wouldn't wash herself if she'd been injured internally. Oh, good Lord!"

He stretched, threw his jacket on the bed and came over to Camille.

"What a fright. How pretty you look, all in white. Kiss me, my fly in the milk!"

She let herself fall into the arms which had remembered her at last and could not hold back some broken sobs.

"No? You're actually crying?"

He was upset himself and hid his forehead in the soft, black hair.

"I . . . I didn't know that you were kind."

She had the courage not to draw away from him at that. However, Alain quickly returned to Saha whom he wanted to take out on the balcony because of the heat. But the cat resisted and contented herself with lying near the open door, turned towards the evening blue, as herself. From time to time, she gave a brief shudder and looked anxiously into the triangular room behind her.

"It's the shock," explained Alain. "I wanted her to go and sit outside."

"Leave her alone," said Camille faintly, "since she doesn't want to."

"Her wishes are orders. Today, of all days! Is there likely to be anything eatable left over at this hour? It's half-past nine!"

Mother Buque wheeled the table out on to the balcony and they dined looking over the east side of Paris where the most lights glimmered. Alain talked a lot, drank water with a little wine in it and accused Saha of clumsiness, imprudence and "cat's sins".

" 'Cat's sins' are the kind of playful mistakes and lapses of judgment which can be put down to their having been civilised and domesticated. They've nothing in common with the clumsiness and carelessness that are almost deliberate."

But Camille no longer asked him: "How do you know that?" After dinner, he carried Saha and drew Camille into the studio where the cat consented to drink the milk she had refused. As she drank, she shivered all over as cats do when they are given something too cold to drink.

"It's the shock," Alain repeated. "All the same, I shall ask Chéron to look in and see her tomorrow morning. Oh, I'm forgetting everything!" he cried gaily. "Will you 'phone the concierge? I've left that roll of plans down in his lodge. The one that Massart, our precious furnishing chap, deposited there."

Camille obeyed while Alain, tired and relaxed after the strain, dropped into one of the scattered armchairs and closed his eyes.

"Hallo!" said Camille at the telephone. "Yes... That must be it. A big roll...Thanks so much."

He laughed with his eyes still closed. She had returned to his side and stood there, watching him laugh.

"That absurd little voice you put on! What is this new little voice? 'A big roll...Thanks so much'," he mimicked. "Do you keep that extremely small voice for the concierge? Come here, it needs the two of us to face Massart's latest creations."

He unrolled a sheet of thick drawing-paper, on the ebony table. Saha, who loved all kinds of paper, promptly leapt on the tinted drawing.

"Isn't she sweet!" exclaimed Alain. "It's to show me she's not in the least hurt. O my miraculously escaped one! Hasn't she a bump on her head? Camille, feel her head. No, she hasn't a bump. Feel her head all the same, Camille."

A poor little murderess meekly tried to emerge from her banishment, stretched out her hand and touched the cat's head with humble hatred.

Her gesture was received with the most savage snarl, a scream and an epileptic leap. Camille shrieked "Ha!" as if she had been burned. Standing on the unrolled drawing the cat covered the young woman with a flaming stare of accusation; the fur on her back erect, her teeth bared and the dry red of her open jaw showing.

Alain had sprung up, ready to protect Saha and Camille from each other.

"Take care! She's...perhaps she's mad... Saha!"

She stared at him angrily but with a lucidity that proved she had not lost her reason.

"What happened? Where did you touch her?"

"I didn't touch her at all."

They were both speaking low, hardly moving their lips.

"Then, why this?" said Alain. "I don't understand. Put your hand out again."

"No, I don't want to!" protested Camille. "Perhaps she's gone wild," she added.

Alain took the risk of stroking Saha. She flattened her erect fur and yielded to the friendly palm but glared once more at Camille with brilliant, accusing eyes.

"Why *this*?" Alain repeated slowly. "Look, she's got a scratch on her nose. I hadn't seen it. It's dried blood. Saha, Saha, good now," he said, seeing the fury growing in the yellow eyes.

Because her cheeks were swelled out and her whiskers stiffly thrust forward as if she were hunting, the furious cat seemed to be laughing. The joy of battle stretched the mauve corners of her mouth and tautened the mobile, muscular chin. The whole of her feline face was striving towards a universal language, towards a word forgotten by men.

"Whatever's *that*?" said Alain suddenly.

"Whatever's *what*?"

Under the cat's stare Camille was recovering her courage and the instinct of self-defence. Leaning over the drawing, Alain could make out damp prints in groups of four little spots round a central, irregular patch.

"Her paws...wet?" muttered Alain.

"She must have walked in some water," said Camille. "You're making a fuss about nothing."

Alain raised her head towards the dry blue night. "In water? What water?"

He turned again to his wife. He looked at her with round eyes which made him look suddenly extraordinarily ugly.

"Don't you know what those footprints mean?" he said harshly. "No, *you* wouldn't know. Fear, d'you understand, *fear*. The sweat of fear. Cat's sweat, the only time cats *do* sweat. So she was frightened."

Delicately, he lifted one of Saha's front paws and dried the sweat on the fleshy pad. Then he pulled back the living white sheath into which the claws had been drawn back.

"She's got all her claws broken," he said, talking to himself. "She must have held on...clutching. She scratched the stone trying to save herself. She..."

He broke off his monologue and, without another word, took the cat under his arm and carried her off to the bathroom.

Alone, unmoving, Camille strained her ears. She kept her hands knotted together; free as she was, she seemed to be loaded with fetters.

"Madame Buque," said Alain's voice, "have you any milk?"

"Yes, Monsieur. In the 'fridge."

"Then it's ice-cold?"

"But I can warm it on the stove. It won't take a second. Is it for the cat? She's not ill, is she?"

"No, she's..."

Alain's voice stopped short and changed its tone: "She's a little off meat in this heat. Thank you, Madame Buque. Yes, you can go now. See you in the morning."

Camille heard her husband moving to and fro and turning on a tap. She knew that he was giving the cat food and fresh water. A diffused shadow, above the metal lampshade, came up as high as her face which was as still as a mask except for the slow movement of the great eyes.

Alain returned, carelessly tightening his leather belt, and sat down again at the ebony table. But he did not summon Camille back to sit beside him and she was forced to speak first.

"You've sent old Mother Buque off?"

"Yes. Shouldn't I have?"

He lit a cigarette and squinted at the flame of the lighter.

"I wanted her to bring something tomorrow morning. Oh, it doesn't matter a bit...don't apologise."

"But I'm not apologising. Though, actually, I ought to."

He went over to the open bay window, drawn by the blue of the night. He was studying a certain tremor in himself, a tremor which did not come from his recent emotion, but which was more like the tremolo of an orchestra, muffled and foreboding. From the Folie-Saint-James a rocket shot up, burst into luminous petals that withered one by one as they fell and the blue of the night recovered its peace and its powdery depth. In the amusement

park, a grotto, a colonnade and a waterfall were suddenly lit up with incandescent white; Camille came nearer to him.

"Are they having a gala night? Let's wait for the fireworks. Do you hear the guitars?"

Absorbed in his inner tremor, he did not answer her. His wrists and hands were tingling, his loins were weak and felt as if a thousand insects were crawling over them. His state reminded him of the hateful lassitude, the fatigue he used to feel after the school sports. After running and rowing he would emerge vindictive; throbbing and exhausted and equally contemptuous of his victory or defeat. Now, he was at peace only in that part of himself which was no longer anxious about Saha. For several minutes—or perhaps for very few—ever since the discovery of the broken claws, ever since Saha's furious terror, he had lost all sense of time.

"It's not fireworks," he said. "Probably just some dances."

From the movement Camille made beside him in the shadow, he realised that she had given up expecting him to answer her. He felt her come closer without apprehension. He saw the outline of the white dress; a bare arm; a half-face lit by the yellow light from the lamps indoors and a half-face that showed blue in the clear night. The two halves were divided by the small straight nose and each was provided with a large, almost unblinking eye.

"Yes, of course, it's dances," she agreed. "They're mandolines, not guitars. Listen..."*Les donneurs...de sé-é-réna...des, Et les bel-les é-écou-teu...*"

Her voice cracked on the highest note and she coughed to excuse her failure.

'But what a tiny voice...' thought Alain, astonished. 'What has she done with her voice that's as big and open as her eyes? She's singing in a little girl's voice. Hoarse, too.'

The mandolines stopped and the breeze brought a faint human noise of clapping and applause. A moment later, a rocket shot up, burst into an umbrella of mauve rays in which hung tears of living fire.

"Oh!" cried Camille.

Both of them had emerged from the darkness like two statues; Camille in lilac marble; Alain whiter, with his hair greenish and his eyes almost colourless. When the rocket had gone out, Camille sighed.

"It never lasts long enough," she said plaintively.

The distant music started again. But the capricious wind deadened the sound of the stringed instruments into a vague shrill buzzing and carried the blasts of the accompanying brass, on two notes, loudly and insistently right into their ears.

"What a shame," said Camille. "They've probably got a frightfully good jazz band. That's *'Love in the Night'* they're playing."

She hummed the tune in a high, shaky, almost inaudible voice, as if she had just been crying. This new voice of hers acutely increased Alain's disquiet. It induced in him a need for revelation, a desire to break down whatever it was that—a long time ago or only a moment ago?—had risen between himself and Camille. It was something to which he could not yet give a name but which was growing fast; something which prevented him from putting his arm round her neck like a boy; something which kept him motionless at her side, alert and expectant, against the wall still warm from the heat of the day. Turning impatient, he said: "Go on singing."

A long red, white and blue shower, falling like the branches of a weeping willow, streaked the sky over the park and showed Alain a Camille, startled and already defiant: "Singing what?"

"Love in the Night or anything else. It doesn't matter what."

She hesitated, then refused.

"Let me listen to the jazz...even from here you can hear it's simply marvellous."

He did not insist. He restrained his impatience and mastered the tingling which had now spread over his entire body.

A swarm of gay little suns, revolving brightly against the darkness, took flight. Alain secretly confronted them with the constellations of his favourite dreams.

'Those are the one to remember. I'll try and take them with me down there,' he noted gravely. 'I've neglected my dreams too much.' At last, in the sky over the Folie, there rose and expanded a kind of straying pink and yellow dawn which burst into vermilion discs and fiery ferns and ribbons of blinding metal.

The shouts of children on the lower balconies greeted this miraculous display. By its light, Alain saw a Camille absent and remote, absorbed in other lights and her own mind.

As soon as the night closed in again, his hesitation vanished and he slipped his own bare arm under Camille's. As he touched that bare arm, he fancied he could see it; its whiteness hardly tinged by the summer and clothed in a fine down that lay flat on the skin, reddish-brown on the forearm, paler near the shoulder.

"You're cold," he murmured. "You're not feeling ill?"

She began to cry very quietly and so promptly that Alain suspected she had been preparing her tears.

"No. It's you. It's you who...who don't love me."

He leant back against the wall and drew Camille against his hip. He could feel her trembling, and cold from her shoulders to her knees, bare above her rolled stockings. She clung to him faithfully, leaning all her weight on him.

"Aha, so I don't love you. Right! Is this another jealousy scene on account of Saha."

He felt a muscular tremor run through the whole of the body he was supporting, a renewal of energy and self-defence. Encouraged by the moment, by a kind of indescribable opportunism, he insisted: "Instead of adopting this charming animal, like me. Are we the only young couple who have a cat or a dog? Would you like a parrot or a marmoset—a pair of doves—a dog, to make me very jealous in my turn?"

She shook her shoulders, protesting with annoyance through closed lips. With his head high, Alain carefully controlled his own voice and egged himself on. 'Go on, a few more bits of nonsense; fill her up and we'll get somewhere. She's like a jar that I've got to turn upside down to empty. Go on. Go on.'

"Would you like a little lion . . . or a baby crocodile of barely fifty? No? Come on, you'd much better adopt Saha. If you'd just take the least bit of trouble, you'd soon see. . . ."

Camille wrenched herself out of his arms so violently that he staggered.

"No!" she cried. *"That,* never! Do you hear me? *Never!"*

"Ah, now we've got it!" Alain said to himself with delight. He pushed Camille into the room, pulled down the outer blind, lit up the rectangle of glass in the ceiling and shut the window. With an animal movement, Camille rushed over to the window and Alain opened it again.

"On condition you don't scream," he said.

He wheeled the only armchair up to Camille and sat astride on the solitary chair at the foot of the wide, turned-down bed with its new, clean sheets. The oilcloth curtains, drawn for the night, gave a greenish cast to Camille's pale face and her creased white dress.

"Well?" began Alain. "No compromise possible? Appalling story? Either her or me?"

She answered with a brief nod and Alain realised that he must drop his bantering tone.

"What do you want me to say?" he went on, after

a silence. "The only thing I don't want to say to you? You know very well I'll never give up this cat. I should be ashamed to. Ashamed in myself and ashamed before her."

"I know," said Camille.

"And before you," Alain finished.

"Oh, *me*!" said Camille, raising her hand.

"You count too," said Alain hardly. "Tell me. Is it only me you've anything against? You've no reproach against Saha except her affection for me?"

She answered only with a troubled, hesitant look and he was irritated at having to go on questioning her. He had thought that a short, violent scene would force all the issues; he had relied on this easy way out. But, after her one cry, Camille had stiffened defensively and was furnishing no fuel for a quarrel. He resorted to patience: "Tell me, my dear. What is it? Mustn't I call you my dear? Tell me, if it were a question of another cat and not Saha, would you be so intolerant?"

"Of course I wouldn't," she said very quickly. "You wouldn't love it as much as that one."

"Quite true," said Alain with loyal accuracy.

"Even a woman," went on Camille, beginning to get heated, "you probably wouldn't love a *woman* as much as that."

"Quite true," said Alain.

"You're not like most people who are fond of animals. No, you're *not*. Patrick's fond of animals. He takes big dogs by the scruff of their necks and rolls them over. He imitates cats to see the faces they make—he whistles to the birds."

"Quite. In other words, he's not difficult," said Alain.

"But you're quite different. You *love* Saha."

"I've never pretended not to. But I wasn't lying to you, either, when I said to you: 'Saha's not your rival.'"

He broke off and lowered his eyelids over his secret which was a secret of purity.

"There are rivals *and* rivals," said Camille sarcastically.

Suddenly she reddened. Flushed with sudden intoxication, she advanced to Alain.

"I saw the two of you!" she almost shrieked. "In the morning, when you spend the night on your little divan. Before daybreak, I've seen you, both of you."

She pointed a shaking hand towards the balcony.

"Sitting there, the two of you . . . you didn't ever hear me! You were like that, cheek to cheek."

She went over to the window, recovered her breath and marched down on Alain again.

"It's for you to say honestly whether I'm wrong in being jealous of this cat and wrong in suffering."

He kept silence so long that she became angry again.

"Do speak! Do *say* something! At the point we've got to . . . What are you waiting for?"

"The sequel," said Alain. "The rest."

He stood up quietly, bent over his wife and lowered his voice as he indicated the french window: "It was you, wasn't it? You threw her over?"

With a swift movement she put the bed between herself and him but she did not deny it. He watched her escape with a kind of smile: "You threw her over," he said dreamily. "I felt very definitely that you'd changed everything between us. You threw her over . . . she broke her claws trying to clutch on to the wall."

He lowered his head, imagining the attempted murder.

"But *how* did you throw her over? By holding her by the skin of her neck? By taking advantage of her being asleep on the parapet? Had you been planning this for a long time? You hadn't had a fight with each other first?"

He raised his head and stared at Camille's hands and arms.

"No, you've no marks. She accused you well and truly, didn't she, when I made you touch her? She was magnificent."

His eyes left Camille and embraced the night, the dust of stars, the tops of the three poplars which the lights in the room lit up.

"Very well," he said simply, "I'm going away."

"Oh listen . . . do *listen* . . ." Camille implored wildly, almost in a whisper.

Nevertheless, she let him go out of the room. He opened cupboards, talked to the cat in the bathroom. The sound of his footsteps warned Camille that he had changed into his outdoor shoes and she looked, automatically, at the time. He came in again, carrying Saha in a bulging basket which Mme. Buque used for shopping. Hurriedly dressed, with his hair dishevelled and a scarf round his neck, his untidiness so much suggested that of a lover that Camille's eyelids pricked. But she heard Saha moving in the basket and tightened her lips.

"As you see, I'm going away," repeated Alain. He lowered his eyes, lifted the basket a trifle and corrected himself with calculated cruelty. "*We're* going away."

He secured the wicker lid, explaining as he did so: "This was all I could find in the kitchen."

"You're going to your home?" inquired Camille, forcing herself to imitate Alain's calm.

"But of course."

"Are you . . . can I count on seeing you during the next few days?"

"Why, certainly."

Surprise made her weaken again. She had to make an immense effort not to plead, not to weep.

"'What about you?" said Alain. "Will you stay here alone tonight? You won't be frightened? If you insisted, I'd stay, but . . .'"

He turned his head towards the balcony.

"But, frankly, I'm not keen on it. What do you propose to say to your family?"

Hurt at his sending her, by implication, home to her people, Camille pulled herself together.

"I've nothing to say to them. These are things which only concern *me*, I presume. I've no inclination for family councils."

"I entirely agree with you . . . provisionally."

"Anyway, we can decide as from tomorrow."

He raised his free hand to ward off this threat of a future.

"No. Not tomorrow. Today there isn't any tomorrow."

In the doorway, he turned back.

"In the bathroom, you'll find my key and all the money we've got here."

She interrupted with irony: "Why not a hamper of provisions and a compass?"

She was putting on a brave act and surveyed him with one hand on her hip and her head erect on her handsome neck. 'She's building up my exit,' thought Alain. He wanted to reply with some similar last-minute coquetry, to toss his hair over his forehead and give her that narrowed look between his lashes which seemed to disdain what it rested on. But he renounced a pantomime which would look absurd when he was carrying a shopping-basket and confined himself to a vague bow in Camille's direction.

She kept up her expression of bravado and her theatrical stance. But before he went out, he could see more clearly, at a distance, the dark circles round her eyes and the moisture which covered her temples and her smooth, unlined neck.

EPITAPH

Here lies Bélaud, my little gray cat:
Bélaud, that was the most handsome perhaps
That Nature ever made in cat's clothing:
This was Bélaud, Death to Rats,
Bélaud, to be sure his beauty was such
That he deserves to be immortal.

Joachim du Ballay

Once upon a time, in a village very far away, there lived an honest and earnest young man. He was a happy person, for he loved his work, which was caring for all the sick animals in the surrounding countryside, and he loved his wife, who was good and sweet and kind. Their life seemed perfect—he cared for the animals, she cared for him, and they were destined to live happily ever after.

Their trouble began in the seventh year of their marriage. The young man had befriended a beautiful black cat, a stray who had wandered into the village one stormy night. The cat refused to come and live with him; instead she accompanied him on his rounds every day and then disappeared for the night to some secret hideaway. Knowing the habits of cats, the young man was not particularly curious about this pattern, although he loved the cat and would have been happy to give her a home. At about this same time, the young man awoke one night to discover that his wife was not beside him. Concerned but exhausted from his day's labor, he dozed again and awoke early in the dawn to notice his wife slipping quietly back into bed beside him.

This strange occurrence repeated itself several nights running. The young man's curiosity turned to anger. He began to suspect his wife. Of what he did not know, but he did find this very suspicious. Finally, he laid a trap. He placed a chain latch on their bedroom door, locked it from within, and went to sleep. Awakened suddenly by his sense that his wife was missing, he rushed to the bolted door, confused and angry with frustration. "How is this possible in the ordinary course of things?" he asked himself. Suddenly he saw something black slipping through the door at his feet. In his consternation, he grabbed a fire poker and slashed at what now looked like a cat's paw. A piercing cry of pain was heard and the paw disappeared.

The young man was bereft. His wife did not return. Many animals were sick, for it was winter and cold, and he worked hard, trying to forget his wife and his grief at her mysterious disappearance. Then, as suddenly as she had disappeared, she reappeared. The young man was overjoyed: he wept with delight. Eventually he realized that his beloved wife was also weeping, but not for joy alone. He embraced her and assured her that nothing anymore in the world was worth crying over now that they were reunited. She tried to smile and sniffle away her tears, but as she reached to touch her husband he gasped in horror. Her hand had been chopped off at the wrist. Anonymous

Jorge Luis Borges

1900-

FICCIONES
(EXCERPT)

At the railroad station he noted that he still had thirty minutes. He quickly recalled that in a cafe on the Calle Brazil (a few dozen feet from Yrigoyen's house) there was an enormous cat which allowed itself to be caressed as if it were a disdainful divinity. He entered the cafe. There was the cat, asleep. He ordered a cup of coffee, slowly stirred the sugar, sipped it (this pleasure had been denied him in the clinic), and thought, as he smoothed the cat's black coat, that this contact was an illusion and that the two beings, man and cat, were as good as separated by a glass, for man lives in time, in succession, while the magical animal lives in the present, in the eternity of the instant....

THE POPE'S CAT

My companion is a large grey and red cat, banded with black. He was born in the Vatican, in the loggia of Raphael. Leo the Twelfth reared him on a fold of his white robe, where I used to look at him with envy when, as ambassador, I received my audiences. The successor of Saint Peter being dead, I inherited the bereaved animal. He is called Micetto, and surnamed 'the Pope's cat,' enjoying in that regard much consideration from pious souls. I endeavour to soften his exile, and help him to forget the Sistine Chapel, and the vast dome of Saint Angelo, where far from earth, he was wont to take his daily promenade. *Chateaubriand*

THE CAT

Within that porch, across the way,
I see two naked eyes this night;
Two eyes that neither shut nor blink,
Searching my face with a green light.

But cats to me are strange, so strange—
I cannot sleep if one is near;
And though I'm sure I see those eyes,
I'm not so sure a body's there! *W. H. Davies*

AN ELEGY
TO OSCAR,
A DEAD CAT

Damn'd be this harsh mechanick age
    That whirls us fast and faster,
And swallows with Sabazian rage
    Nine lives in one disaster.

I take my quill with sadden'd thought,
    Tho' falt'ringly I do it;
And, having curst the Juggernaut,
    Inscribe: OSCARVS FVIT! *H. P. Lovecraft*

OF WALT
WHITMAN

If it be true that all remarkable human beings resemble animals, then Walt Whitman was like a cat —a great grey Angora Tom, alert in response, serenely blinking under his combed waves of hair, with eyes inscrutably dreaming. *Edmund Gosse*

Mark Van Doren

1894-1972

MIDWIFE
CAT

Beyond the fence she hesitates,
    And drops a paw, and tries the dust.
It is a clearing, but she waits
    No longer minute than she must.

Though a dozen foes may dart
    From out the grass, she crouches by,
Then runs to where the silos start
    To heave their shadows far and high.

Here she folds herself and sleeps;
    But in a moment she has put
The dreams aside; and now she creeps
    Across the open, foot by foot,

Till at the threshold of a shed
    She smells the water and the corn
Where a sow is on her bed
    And little pigs are being born.

Silently she leaps, and walks
    All night upon a narrow rafter,
Whence at intervals she talks
    Wise to them she watches after.

William Salmon

17TH CENTURY

THE DIMINUTIVE
LYON OR CATUS,
THE CAT

The cat is bred and is an Inhabitant of almost all Countries in the World, all *Cats* were at first wild, but were at length tamed by the industry of Mankind; it is a Beast of prey, even the tame one, more especially the wild, it being in the opinion of many nothing but a diminutive Lyon.

It has a broad Face almost like a Lyon, short Ears, large Whiskers, shining Eyes, short smooth Hair, long Tail, rough Tongue, and armed on its Feet with Claws, being a crafty, subtle watchful Creature, very loving and familiar with Man-kind, the mortal enemy to the Rat, Mouse, and all sorts of Birds, which it seizes on as its prey. As to its Eyes, Authors say that they shine in the Night, and see better at the full, and more dimly at the change of the Moon; as also that the Cat doth vary his Eyes with the Sun, the Apple of its Eye being long at

Sun rise, round towards Noon, and not to be seen at all at night, but the whole Eye shining in the night. These appearances of the Cats Eyes I am sure are true, but whether they answer to the times of the day, I never observed.

It is a neat and cleanly creature, often licking it self, to keep it fair and clean, and washing its Face with its fore-feet; the best are such as are of a fair and large kind, and of an exquisite Tabby color, called *Cyprus* Cats. They usually generate in the winter Season, making a great noise, go 56 Days or 8 weeks with young, and bring forth 2, 3, 4, 5, 6, or more at a time, they cover their excrements, and love to keep their old habitations.

Oliver Herford

1863-1935

THREE POEMS

Kittens, you are very little,
    And your kitten bones are brittle,
If you'd grow to Cats respected,
    See your play be not neglected.

Smite the Sudden Spool, and spring
    Upon the Swift Elusive String,
Thus you learn to catch the wary
    Mister Mouse or Miss Canary.

But the Kittencats who snatch
    Rudely for their food, or scratch,
Grow to Tomcats gaunt and gory,—
    Theirs is quite another story.

Cats like these are put away
    By the dread S.P.C.A.
Or to trusting Aunts and Sisters
    Sold as sable Muffs and Wristers.

———————

When Human Folk at Table eat,
    A Kitten must not mew for meat,
Or jump to grab it from the Dish,
    (Unless it happens to be fish).

———————

To Someone very Good and Just,
    Who has proved worthy of her trust,
A Cat will sometimes condescend—
    The Dog is Everybody's friend.

Mikhail Bulgakov

1891-1940

THE MASTER
AND MARGARITA
(EXCERPTS)

Ivan gasped, looked up and saw the hateful stranger in the distance. He was already at the exit to Patriarchs' Lane, and he was not alone. The more than dubious choirmaster had already managed to join him. But this was not all. There was a third member of this company, who had appeared from heaven knows where: a tom cat, huge as a hog, black as pitch or a crow, and with a huge mustache, for all the world like a rakish cavalryman's. The trio marched off into Patriarchs' Lane, the tom cat walking on his hind legs.

Ivan hurried after the malefactors, but he saw at once that it would be difficult to catch up with them.

The trio dashed through the lane in an instant and was emerging on Spiridonovka. No matter how much Ivan increased his pace, the distance between him and those he pursued never diminished. Before he knew it, he was out of the quiet Spiridonovka and at the Nikitsky Gate. And here the milling crowds made his position still more hopeless. Besides, the criminal band resorted to the favorite stratagem of thieves, and scattered.

The choirmaster nimbly whirled himself into a bus speeding toward Arbat Square and disappeared. Having lost one of the gang, Ivan concentrated his attention on the tom cat and saw how this strange tom walked over to the boarding step of an "A" streetcar waiting at the stop, brazenly elbowed aside a woman who squealed as she saw him, grasped the hand rails and even attempted to give the conductor a coin through the window, which was open because of the heat.

The tom's behavior struck Ivan with such amazement that he stopped transfixed near the grocery store on the corner. And now he was struck again, even more forcibly, by the behavior of the woman conductor. As soon as she saw the tom trying to climb into the streetcar, she screamed, trembling with rage:

"No cats allowed here! Nobody with cats allowed! Scram! Get off, or I'll call the militia!"

Neither the conductor, nor the passengers were as astounded by the situation itself—a cat climbing into a streetcar!—which would not have been half so bad, as by his wish to pay his fare!

The tom, it turned out, was not only a solvent, but also a disciplined beast. At the conductor's first cry, he ceased his advance, got down from the step, and sat down at the stop, rubbing his whisker with the coin. But as soon as the conductor pulled the cord and the cars started, the tom proceeded to do what anyone else would who had been expelled from a streetcar but must nevertheless get to his destination. Allowing all three cars to go by, the tom jumped up onto the rear of the last one, sank his claws into a rubber tube projecting from the wall, and rode away, thus saving himself the fare.

———————

A third visitor sprawled insolently on the padded ottoman that had once belonged to the jeweler's lady—namely, a black tom of terrifying proportions, with a glass of vodka in one paw and a fork in the other with which he had already managed to impale a pickled mushroom.

The dim light in the bedroom began to fade out altogether in Styopa's eyes. "So that's how people lose their minds. . . ." he thought and caught at the doorpost.

"I see that you are a little surprised, my dearest Stepan Bogdanovich?" Woland inquired of Styopa who stared at the room with chattering teeth. "But there is nothing to wonder at. This is my retinue."

The tom emptied his glass of vodka, and Styopa's hand began to slide down the doorpost.

"And this retinue requires space," continued Woland. "So that we have one too many in the apartment. And it seems to me that the one is you."

"They, they!" the lanky checkered character bleated like a goat, referring to Styopa in the plural. "Generally, they've been behaving like a dreadful swine lately. Drinking, having affairs with women on the strength of their position in the theater, not doing a stitch of work and really incapable of doing any, since they don't know the first thing about the job. Putting things over on their superiors!"

"Using the government car for nothing," the tom tattled as he chewed his mushroom.

———————

Besides the people in the room, there was also

an enormous black tom who sat on a high stool before the chess table, with a knight in his right paw.

Hella rose slightly and bowed to Margarita. The tom jumped off the stool and did the same. As he scraped with his hind paw, he dropped the knight and crawled under the bed to recover it...

"I cannot find the knight," the tom replied from under the bed in a muffled false voice. "He galloped off somewhere, and I keep picking up some infernal frog."

"Do you imagine that you are at a fair in some market place?" Woland pretended to be angry. "There are no frogs under the bed! Leave those cheap tricks for the Variety Theater. If you don't come out at once, we shall regard the game as conceded, you damned deserter!"

"Never, Messire!" the tom yelled and immediately crawled out from under the bed with the knight in his paw.

"May I present to you . . ." Woland began, and interrupted himself: "No, I can't stand this clown. Look what he did to himself under the bed!"

The tom, covered with dust and standing on his hind legs, was in the meantime bowing to Margarita. Now he had a white evening bow tie around his neck; a ladies' mother-of-pearl opera glass dangled from a ribbon on his chest. Besides, his whiskers were gilded.

"What's this now?" cried Woland. "Why did you gild your whiskers? And why the devil do you need a tie if you have no trousers?"

"A cat isn't supposed to wear trousers, Messire," the tom answered with great dignity. "You will tell me to put on boots next! Puss in Boots exists only in fairy tales, Messire. But have you ever seen anyone at a ball without a tie? I don't intend to make myself a laughing stock and risk being kicked out! Everyone adorns himself as best he can. You may consider this as applying to the opera glass, Messire!"

"But the whiskers? . . ."

"I don't understand," the tom objected drily. "Why could Azazello and Koroviev put white powder on their faces after shaving today, and in what way is white powder better than gold? I powdered my whiskers, that's all! It would be different if I had shaved! A shaven tom would indeed be outrageous, I agree a thousand times. But generally," and the tom's voice trembled with injured feelings, "I see that people are picking on me. I see that I am facing a serious problem: am I to attend the ball at all? What will you say to that, Messire?"

And the tom puffed himself up with chagrin to such a size that it seemed he would burst in another second.

"Oh, you swindler, you swindler," Woland said, shaking his head. "Every time he is about to lose a game, he'll try to pull the wool over your eyes, like the worst charlatan. Sit down at once and stop your jabbering."

———————

"What are those steps on the staircase?" asked Koroviev, playing with his spoon in the cup of black coffee.

"Oh, they're coming to arrest us," answered Azazello and drank down a glass of cognac.

"Ah...well, well..." answered Koroviev.

In the meantime, the men who were climbing up the front staircase were already on the third floor landing. Two plumbers were busy there, repairing the steam radiator. The men and the plumbers exchanged knowing glances.

The man in front openly took a black Mauser from under his coat, and the one next to him prepared his passkeys. Generally, the group advancing on apartment Number 50 was properly equipped. Two of the men had fine, easily opened silk nets in their pockets. Another had a lasso, and still another, cheesecloth masks and ampules with chloroform.

The front door to apartment Number 50 was opened in a second, and all the visitors piled into the foyer. The door slammed in the kitchen at that moment indicated that the other group had also arrived.

This time they met, if not with a full, at least with a partial success. Men scattered instantly through all the rooms and found no one anywhere, but in the dining room they discovered the remnants of a breakfast that had obviously been hastily abandoned, and on the mantelpiece in the parlor, next to the crystal vase, they saw a huge black tom. He held a primus stove in his paws.

The visitors contemplated the tom in total silence for a long time.

"Mmm, yes...that's a good one..." whispered one of the men.

"I'm doing no mischief, I don't bother any one, I'm repairing the primus," the tom said frigidly, with a scowl. "And I must warn you that a cat is an ancient and inviolable animal."

"Extraordinarily clean work," whispered one of the men, and another said loudly and clearly:

"Well, then, inviolable and ventriloquist tom, come over here!"

A net unfolded and flew up, but, to everyone's astonishment, it missed and caught only the vase, which fell crashing on the floor.

"Forfeit!" yelled the tom. "Hurrah!" And, putting aside the primus, he seized a Browning from behind his back. He aimed it instantly at the nearest man, but before the tom managed to fire, the gun in the man's hand flashed, and the tom tumbled head down on the floor, dropping the Browning and also bringing the primus after him.

"It's all over," the tom said in a weak voice and sprawled languidly in the puddle of blood. "Step aside for a moment, let me say good-by to the earth. Ah, my friend Azazello," the tom moaned, bleeding profusely, "where art thou? Thou hast not come to my aid in the unequal battle, thou hast abandoned poor Behemoth, exchanging him for a glass of cognac—very good cognac, it must be said! Oh, well, then, let my death be on thy conscience, I bequeath my Browning to thee. . . ."

"The net, the net. . . ." The men around the tom whispered. But the net for some unknown reason, had got caught in someone's pocket and refused to be extracted.

"The only thing that can save the mortally wounded tom," said the tom, "is a sip of benzine." And, taking advantage of the delay, he put his lips to the round opening in the primus stove and gulped down some benzine. Immediatly the blood stopped gushing from his upper left paw. The tom sprang up, alive and merry, caught the primus under his arm, and leaped up to the mantel. Then, ripping the wallpaper, he clambered up the wall and two seconds later was sitting on the metal cornice over the window, high above the visitors.

Hands seized the drapes and tore them down together with the cornice. The sun flooded the dim room. But neither the shamming tom, nor the primus stove fell on the floor. Without letting the primus go, the tom managed to swing across the air and alight on the chandelier hanging in the center of the room.

"A stepladder!" someone cried below.

"I challenge you to a duel!" bawled the tom, flying over the heads of the men on the swinging chandelier, and now again he had a Browning in his paws, having found a spot for the primus in the branches of the chandelier. The tom took aim and opened fire, flying like a pendulum over the visitors. The blasts shook the apartment. Crystal splinters hailed on the floor, the mirror over the mantel blossomed with stars, plaster dust filled the air, empty cartridge cases bounced on the floor, the windowpanes cracked, a jet of benzine shot out of a bullet hole in the primus.

However, the skirmish was brief and the firing soon died down by itself. The point is that neither the tom, nor the visitors suffered any ill effects from it. No one was killed; in fact, no one was even wounded. Everyone was safe and sound. To make entirely sure, one of the visitors sent five bullets straight at the head of the damned animal, and the tom promptly emptied a whole cartridge clip in reply. But the same thing happened—the bullets produced no effect whatsoever. The tom swayed on the chandelier in constantly diminishing arcs, for some reason blowing into the muzzle of the Browning and spitting on his paw.

The faces of the men below expressed utter bafflement. This was the only, or one of the only, cases when bullets were entirely without effect. Of course, it might have been assumed that the tom's Browning was only a toy, but this certainly could not be said of the visitors' Mausers. As for the tom's first wound, it was entirely clear that it was nothing but a trick and shameless faking, as was his pretense at drinking benzine.

They made another attempt to capture the tom, using a lasso. But it caught one of the lamps, and the chandelier crashed down, shaking—it seemed—the whole building, and still without result. The men were showered with flying splinters, while the tom flew across the air and settled on top of the gilded frame of the mantelpiece mirror, right under the ceiling. He showed no intention of escaping anywhere, but, sitting in relative safety, launched into another speech:

"I am totally at a loss to understand," he said from his perch, "the reasons why I am being treated so rudely. . . ."

At this point, his speech was interrupted by a heavy low voice coming from heaven knows where:

"What's going on in this house? They don't let me work. . . ."

Another voice, nasal and unpleasant, answered:

"But, of course, it's Behemoth, the devil take him!"

A third, quavering voice said:

"Messire! It is the Sabbath. The sun is sinking. Time for us to go."

"Forgive me, I cannot talk to you any more," said the tom from the mirror. "It's time for us to go." He threw his Browning and shattered both panes in the window. Then he splashed the benzine, and it flared up by itself, sending up a wave of flame to the ceiling.

The blaze spread with unusual speed and violence, rare even with the use of benzine. The wallpaper immediately began to smoke, flames rose from the drapery on the floor, and the window frames began to smolder. The tom poised himself

for a leap, miaowed, swung from the mirror to the window sill and vanished together with his primus. Shots were heard outside. A man sitting on the iron fire escape on the level of the apartment windows sprayed the tom with bullets as he flew from window sill to window sill toward the drainpipe at the corner of the building, then clambered up the pipe to the roof. There he was fired on—unfortunately, equally without effect—by the guards stationed at the chimneys, and disappeared in the light of the setting sun which was flooding the city at that hour.

Excerpts, translated by Mirra Ginsburg

93

Anne Frank

THE DIARY
OF ANNE FRANK

Wednesday, 10 May, 1944

We were sitting in the attic doing some French yesterday afternoon when I suddenly heard water pattering down behind me. I asked Peter what it could be, but he didn't even reply, simply tore up to the loft, where the source of the disaster was, and pushed Mouschi, who, because of the wet earth box, had sat down beside it, harshly back to the right place. A great din and disturbance followed, and Mouschi, who had finished by that time, dashed downstairs.

Mouschi, seeking the convenience of something similar to his box, had chosen some wood shavings. The pool had trickled down from the loft into the attic immediately and, unfortunately, landed just beside and in the barrel of potatoes. The ceiling was dripping, and as the attic floor is not free from holes either, several yellow drips came through the ceiling into the dining room between a pile of stockings and some books, which were lying on the table. I was doubled up with laughter, it really was a scream. There was Mouschi crouching under a chair, Peter with water, bleaching powder, and floor cloth, and Van Daan trying to soothe everyone. The calamity was soon over, but it's a well-known fact that cats' puddles positively stink. The potatoes proved this only too clearly and also the wood shavings, that Daddy collected in a bucket to be burned. Poor Mouschi! How were you to know that peat is unobtainable?

Leigh Hunt

1784-1850

THE CAT
BY THE FIRE

Poor Pussy! she looks up at us again, as if she thanked us for those vindications of dinner; and symbolically gives a twist of a yawn and a lick of her whiskers. Now she proceeds to clean herself all over, having a just sense of the demands of her elegant person—beginning judiciously with her paws, and fetching amazing tongues at her hind-hips. Anon, she scratches her neck with a foot of rapid delight, leaning her head towards it, and shutting her eyes, half to accommodate the action of the skin, and half to enjoy the luxury. She then rewards her paws with a few more touches; look at the action of her head and neck, how pleasing it is, the ears pointed forward, and the neck gently arching to and fro. Finally, she gives a sneeze, and another twist of mouth and whiskers, and then, curling her tail towards her front claws, settles herself on her hind quarters, in an attitude of bland meditation . . .

Tennessee Williams

1914-

THE MALEDICTION

In the evenings, with Nitchevo the cat, he could shut it partly away. Nitchevo's presence was a denial of all the many threatening elements of chance. You could see that Nitchevo did not take stock in chance. She believed that everything progressed according to a natural, predestined order and that there was nothing to be apprehensive about. All of her movements were slow and without agitation. They were accomplished with a consumate grace. Her amber eyes regarded each object with unblinkling serenity. Even about her food she made no haste. Each evening Lucio brought home a pint of milk for her supper and breakfast: Nitchevo sat quietly waiting on her haunches while he poured it into the cracked saucer borrowed from the landlady and set it on the floor beside the bed. Then he lay down on the bed, expectantly watching, while Nitchevo came slowly forward to the pale blue saucer. She looked up at him once—slowly—with her unflickering yellow eyes before she started to eat, and then she gracefully lowered her small chin to the saucer's

edge, the red satin tip of tongue protruded and the room was filled with the sweet, faint music of her gently lapping....

An excerpt

Observe a cat entering a room for the first time: it searches and smells about, it is not quiet for a moment, it trusts nothing until it has examined and made acquaintance with everything.   *Rousseau*

Saki (H. H. Munro)

1870-1916

TOBERMORY

It was a chill, rain-washed afternoon of the late August day, that indefinite season when partridges are still in security or cold storage, and there is nothing to hunt—unless one is bounded on the north by the Bristol Channel, in which case one may lawfully gallop after fat red stags. Lady Blemley's house-party was not bounded on the north by the Bristol Channel, hence there was a full gathering of her guests round the tea-table on this particular afternoon. And, in spite of the blankness of the season and the triteness of the occasion, there was no trace in the company of that fatigued restlessness which means a dread of the pianola and a subdued hankering for auction bridge. The undisguised open-mouthed attention of the entire party was fixed on the homely negative personality of Mr. Cornelius Appin. Of all her guests, he was the one who had come to Lady Blemley with the vaguest reputation. Someone had said he was "clever", and he had got his invitation in the moderate expectation, on the part of his hostess, that some portion at least of his cleverness would be contributed to the general entertainment. Until tea-time that day she had been unable to discover in what direction, if any, his cleverness lay. He was neither a wit nor a croquet champion, a hypnotic force nor a begetter of amateur theatricals. Neither did his exterior suggest the sort of man in whom women are willing to pardon a generous measure of mental deficiency. He had subsided into mere Mr Appin, and the Cornelius seemed a piece of transparent baptismal bluff. And now he was claiming to have launched on the world a discovery beside which the invention of gunpowder, of the printing press, and of steam locomotion were inconsiderable trifles. Science had made bewildering strides in many directions during recent decades, but this thing seemed to belong to the domain of the miracle rather than to scientific achievement.

"And do you really ask us to believe," Sir Wilfred was saying, "that you have discovered a means for instructing animals in the art of human speech and that dear old Tobermory has proved your first successful pupil?"

"It is a problem at which I have worked for the last seventeen years," said Mr Appin, "but only during the last eight or nine months have I been rewarded with glimmerings of success. Of course I have experimented with thousands of animals, but latterly only with cats, those wonderful creatures which have assimilated themselves so marvellously with our civilization while retaining all their highly developed feral instincts. Here and there among cats one comes across an outstanding superior intellect, just as one does among the ruck of human beings, and when I made the acquaintance of Tobermory a week ago I saw at once that I was in contact with a 'Beyond-cat' of extraordinary intelligence. I had gone far along the road to success in recent experiments; with Tobermory, as you call him, I have reached the goal."

Mr Appin concluded his remarkable statement in a voice which he strove to divest of a triumphant infection. No one said "Rats", though Clovis's lips moved in a monosyllabic contortion which probably invoked those rodents of disbelief.

"And do you mean to say," asked Miss Resker, after a slight pause, "that you have taught Tobermory to say and understand easy sentences of one syllable?"

"My dear Miss Resker," said the wonder-worker patiently, "one teaches little children and savages and backward adults in that piecemeal fashion; when one has solved the problem of making a beginning with an animal of highly developed intelligence one has no need for those halting methods. Tomermory can speak our language with perfect correctness."

This time Clovis very distinctly said, "Beyond-rats!" Sir Wilfred was more polite, but equally skeptical.

"Hadn't we better have the cat in and judge for ourselves?" suggested Lady Blemley.

Sir Wilfred went in search of the animal, and the company settled themselves down to the languid expectation of witnessing some more or less adroit drawing-room ventriloquism.

In a minute Sir Wilfred was back in the room, his face white beneath its tan and eyes dilated with excitement.

"By gad, it's true!"

His agitation was unmistakably genuine, and his hearers started forward in a thrill of awakened interest.

Collapsing into an armchair he continued breathlessly: "I found him dozing in the smoking-room, and called out to him to come for his tea. He blinked at me in his usual way, and I said, 'Come on, Toby; don't keep us waiting'; and, by Gad! he drawled out in a most horribly natural voice that he'd come when he dashed well pleased! I nearly jumped out of my skin!"

Appin had preached to absolutely incredulous hearers; Sir Wilfred's statement carried instant conviction. A Babel-like chorus of startled exclamation arose, amid which the scientist sat mutely enjoying the first fruit of his stupendous discovery.

In the midst of the clamour Tobermory entered the room and made his way with velvet tread and studied unconcern across to the group seated round the tea-table.

A sudden hush of awkwardness and constraint fell upon the company. Somehow there seemed an element of embarrassment in addressing on equal terms a domestic cat of acknowledged mental ability.

"Will you have some milk, Tobermory?" asked Lady Blemley in a rather strained voice.

"I don't mind if I do," was the response, couched in a tone of even indifference. A shiver of suppressed excitement went through the listeners, and Lady Blemley might be excused for pouring out the saucerful of milk rather unsteadily.

"I'm afraid I've spilt a good deal of it," she said apologetically.

"After all, it's not my Axminster," was Tobermory's rejoinder.

Another silence fell on the group, and then Miss Resker, in her best district-visitor manner, asked if the human language had been difficult to learn. Tobermory looked squarely at her for a moment and then fixed his gaze serenely on the middle distance. It was obvious that boring questions lay outside his scheme of life.

"What do you think of human intelligence?" asked Mavis Pellington lamely.

"Of whose intelligence in particular?" asked Tobermory coldly.

"Oh, well, mine for instance," said Mavis, with a feeble laugh.

"You put me in an embarrassing position," said Tobermory, whose tone and attitude certainly did not suggest a shred of embarrassment.

"When your inclusion in this house-party was suggested Sir Wilfred protested that you were the most brainless woman of his acquaintance, and that there was a broad distinction between hospitality and the care of the feeble-minded. Lady Blemley

replied that your lack of brain-power was the precise quality which had earned you your invitation, as you were the only person she could think of who might be idiotic enough to buy their old car. You know, the one they call 'The Envy of Sisyphus', because it goes quite nicely uphill if you push it."

Lady Blemley's protestations would have had greater effect if she had not casually suggested to Mavis only that morning that the car in question would be just the thing for her down at her Devonshire home.

Major Barfield plunged in heavily to effect a diversion.

"How about your carryings-on with the tortoise-shell puss up at the stables, eh?"

The moment he had said it everyone realized the blunder.

"One does not usually discuss these matters in public," said Tobermory frigidly. "From a slight observation of your ways since you've been in this house I should imagine you'd find it inconvenient if I were to shift the conversation on to your own little affairs."

The panic which ensued was not confined to the major.

"Would you like to go and see if cook has got your dinner ready?" suggested Lady Blemley hurriedly, affecting to ignore the fact that it wanted at least two hours to Tobermory's dinner-time.

"Thanks," said Tobermory, "not quite so soon after my tea. I don't want to die of indigestion."

"Cats have nine lives, you know," said Sir Wilfred heartily.

"Possibly," answered Tobermory; "but only one liver."

"Adelaide!" said Mrs Cornett, "do you mean to encourage that cat to go out and gossip about us in the servants' hall?"

The panic had indeed become general. A narrow ornamental balustrade ran in front of most of the bedroom windows at the Towers, and it was recalled with dismay that this had formed a favourite promenade for Tobermory at all hours, whence he could watch the pigeons—and heaven knew what else besides. If he intended to become reminiscent in his present outspoken strain the effect would be something more than disconcerting. Mrs Cornett, who spent much time at her toilet table, and whose complexion was reputed to be of a nomadic though punctual disposition, looked as ill at ease as the Major. Miss Scrawen, who wrote fiercely sensuous poetry and led a blameless life, merely displayed irritation; if you are methodical and virtuous in private you don't necessarily want everyone to know it. Bertie van Tahn, who was so depraved at seventeen that he had long ago given up trying to be any worse, turned a dull shade of gardenia white, but he did not commit the error of dashing out of the room like Odo Finsberry, a young gentleman who was understood to be reading for the Church and who was possibly disturbed at the thought of scandals he might hear concerning other people. Clovis had the presence of mind to maintain a composed exterior; privately he was calculating how long it would take to procure a box of fancy mice through the agency of the *Exchange and Mart* as a species of hush-money.

Even in a delicate situation like the present, Agnes Resker could not endure to remain too long in the background.

"Why did I ever come down here?" she asked dramatically.

Tobermory immediately accepted the opening.

"Judging by what you said to Mrs Cornett on the croquet-lawn yesterday, you were out for food. You described the Blemleys as the dullest people to stay with that you knew, but said they were clever enough to employ a first-rate cook; otherwise they'd find it difficult to get anyone to come down a second time."

"There's not a word of truth in it! I appeal to Mrs Cornett—" exclaimed the discomfited Agnes.

"Mrs Cornett repeated your remark afterwards to Bertie van Tahn," continued Tobermory, and said, "That woman is a regular Hunger Marcher; she'd go anywhere for four square meals a day, and Bertie van Tahn said—"

At this point the chronicle mercifully ceased. Tobermory had caught a glimpse of the big yellow Tom from the Rectory working his way through the shrubbery towards the stable wing. In a flash he had vanished through the open French window.

With the disappearance of his too brilliant pupil Cornelius Appin found himself beset by a hurricane of bitter upbraiding, anxious enquiry, and frightened entreaty. The responsibility for the situation lay with him, and he must prevent matters from becoming worse. Could Tobermory impart his dangerous gift to other cats? was the first question he had to answer. It was possible, he replied, that he might have initiated his intimate friend the stable puss into his new accomplishment, but it was unlikely that his teaching could have taken a wider range as yet.

"Then," said Mrs Cornett, "Tobermory may be a valuable cat and a great pet; but I'm sure you'll agree, Adelaide, that both he and the stable cat must be done away with without delay."

"You don't suppose I've enjoyed the last quarter of an hour, do you?" said Lady Blemley bitterly. "My husband and I are very fond of Tobermory—at least, we were before this horrible accomplishment was infused into him; but now, of course, the only thing is to have him destroyed as soon as possible."

"We can put some strychnine in the scraps he always gets at dinner-time," said Sir Wilfred, "and I will go and drown the stable cat myself. The coachman will be very sore at losing his pet, but I'll say a very catching form of mange has broken out in both cats and we're afraid of it spreading to the kennels."

"But my great discovery!" expostulated Mr Appin; "after all my years of research and experiment—"

"You can go and experiment on the short-horns at the farm, who are under proper control," said Mrs Cornett, "or the elephants at the Zoological Gardens. They're said to be highly intelligent, and they have this recommendation, that they don't come creeping about our bedrooms and under chairs, and so forth."

An archangel ecstatically proclaiming the Millennium, and then finding that it clashed unpardonably with Henley and would have to be indefinitely postponed, could hardly have felt more crestfallen than Cornelius Appin at the reception of his wonderful achievement. Public opinion, however, was against him—in fact, had the general voice been consulted on the matter it is probable that a strong minority would have been in favour of including him in the strychnine diet.

Defective train arrangements and a nervous desire to see matters brought to a finish prevented an immediate dispersal of the party, but dinner that evening was not a social success. Sir Wilfred had had rather a trying time with the stable cat and subsequently with the coachman. Agnes Resker ostentatiously limited her repast to a morsel of dry toast, which she bit as though it were a personal enemy; whilst Mavis Pellington maintained a vindictive silence throughout the meal. Lady Blemley kept up a flow of what she hoped was conversation, but her attention was fixed on the doorway. A plateful of carefully dosed fish scraps was in readiness on the sideboard, but sweets and savoury and dessert went their way, and no Tobermory appeared either in the dining-room or kitchen.

The sepulchral dinner was cheerful compared to the subsequent vigil in the smoking-room. Eating and drinking had at least supplied a distraction and cloak to the prevailing embarrassment. Bridge was

out of the question in the general tension of nerves and tempers, and after Odo Finsberry had given a lugubrious rendering of "Melisande in the Wood" to a frigid audience, music was tacitly avoided. At eleven the servants went to bed, announcing that the small window in the pantry had been left open as usual for Tobermory's private use. The guests read steadily through the current batch of magazines, and fell back gradually on the "Badminton Library" and bound volumes of *Punch*. Lady Blemley made periodic visits to the pantry, returning each time with an expression of listless depression which forestalled questioning.

At two o'clock Clovis broke the dominating silence.

"He won't turn up tonight. He's probably in the local newspaper office at the present moment, dictating the first instalment of his reminiscences. Lady What's-her-name's book won't be in it. It will be the event of the day."

Having made this contribution to the general cheerfulness, Clovis went to bed. At long intervals the various members of the house-party followed his example.

The servants taking round the early tea made a uniform announcement to a uniform question. Tobermory had not returned.

Breakfast was, if anything, a more unpleasant function than dinner had been, but before its conclusion the situation was relieved. Tobermory's corpse was brought in from the shrubbery, where a gardener had just discovered it. From the bites on his throat and the yellow fur which coated his claws it was evident that he had fallen in unequal combat with the big Tom from the Rectory.

By midday most of the guests had quitted the Towers, and after lunch Lady Blemley had sufficiently recovered her spirits to write an extremely nasty letter to the Rectory about the loss of her valuable pet.

Tobermory had been Appin's one successful pupil, and he was destined to have no successor. A few weeks later an elephant in the Dresden Zoological Garden, which had shown no previous signs of irritability, broke loose and killed an Englishman who had apparently been teasing it. The victim's name was variously reported in the papers as Oppin and Eppelin, but his front name was faithfully rendered Cornelius.

"If he was trying German irregular verbs on the poor beast," said Clovis, "he deserved all he got."

Good liquor is enough to make a cat speak. *Proverb*

Gulielmus Baldwin

16TH CENTURY

BEWARE
THE CAT

Once I was in Ireland in the time that Macmorro and all the rest of the wild lords were the King's enemies, during which time mortal strife was between the Fitzhonies and the Prior and Covent of the Abbey of Tinthern, who counted themselves the King's friends and subjects and whose neighbour was Cayn Macort, a wilde Irish man, then the King's enemy and one which daily made inrodes into the county of Washford and burned such towns and carried away all such cattell as he might come by. By means whereof all the country from Climin to Roffe became a wilde wilderness and is scarce recovered unto this day. In this time, I say, as I was on a night at Corberry with one of the Fitzburies' churles, we fell in talk as we have done now, of strange adventures, and of cats; and there, among other things, the churl (for so they call all farmers and husbandmen) told me as ye shall hear.

"There was (not seven years past) a kern of John Butlers dwelling in the county of Bantry called Patrick Apore, who minding to make a prey in the night upon Cager Makent, his master's enemy, got him with his boy, for so they call their horse keepers, even if they be ever so old knaves, into his country, and in the night time entered into a town of two houses, and broke in and slew the people, and then took such cattle as they found, which was a cow and a sheep and departed therewith homewards; but fearing they should be pursued, the cur dogs making such a shrill barking, he got into a church, thinking to lurk there till midnight was past, for he was sure that no one would suspect or seek him, for the wild Irish men have had churches in such reverence (till our men taught them the contrary) that they never would, nor durst, rob aught hence or hurt any man that took the church yard for sanctuary, not even if he had killed his father. And while the kern was in the church, he thought it best to dine for he had eaten little that day, wherefore he made his boy go gather sticks and strike fire with his flints and made a fire in the church, and he killed the sheep and, after the Irish fashion, layed it thereupon and roasted it.

"But when it was ready, and he thought to eat it, there came in a cat who sat herself by him and said in Irish, *Shane foel*, which is, 'Give me some meat'. He, mazed at this, gave her the quarter that was in his hand, which immediately she did eat up, and asked for more till she had consumed all the sheep. And, like a cormorant not satisfied therewith, she asked still for more, whereupon they supposed it were the Devil himself and therefore, thinking it wisdom to please him, killed the cow which they had stolen, and when they had flayed it, gave the cat a quarter which she immediately devoured. Then they gave her two quarters and, in the meanwhile, after their native fashion, they did cut a piece of the hide and prickt it upon four stakes which they set about the fire, and therein they placed a piece of the cow for themselves, and with the rest of the hide they made each of them bags to wear about their feet, like brogues, both to keep their feet from hurt all the next day, and also to serve for meat the next night, by boyling them upon coals, if they could get none other.

"By this time, the cat had eaten three quarters and called for more, wherefore they gave that which was a-seething by the fire and doubting lest

when she had eaten that she would eat them too, because they had no more for her, they got themselves out of the chuch, and the kern took his horse and away he rode as fast as he could hie. When he was a mile or two from the church the moon began to shine and the boy espied the cat upon his master's horse behind him, whereupon the kern took his dart and, turning his face towards her, flung it and struck her through with it. But immediately there came such a hoarde of cats that after a long fight with them his boy was killed and eaten up and he himself (as good and swift as his horse was) had much to do to escape.

"When he was come home, all weary and hungry, and had put off his harness, which was a corset of mail and like a shirt, and his helmet, which was gilt leather and crested with other skin, he sat himself down by his wife and told her his adventure—upon hearing which the kitten which his wife kept, scarce half a year old, started up and said, 'Hast thou killed Grimallykin?' and straightway plunged in his face and with her teeth took him by the throat and, ere she could be plucked away, she had strangled him."

Told by Michel Parry, 1972

Alexandre Dumas

1802-1870

MYSOUFF

We lived in the Rue de l'Ouest, and we had a cat called Mysouff. The animal had clearly missed its vocation; it ought to have been born a dog. . . . The instant that he caught sight of me, he began lashing the pavement with his tail; then as I came nearer and nearer, he would get to his feet . . . tail held high and back arched. The moment I set foot in the Rue de l'Ouest, he used to dance about my feet like a dog. Then frisking along in front, and turning back to rejoin me, he would start back for the house. Twenty yards from the door, he would come back for a last look and then dash in, in full gallop. Two seconds later I would see my mother appear on the threshold.

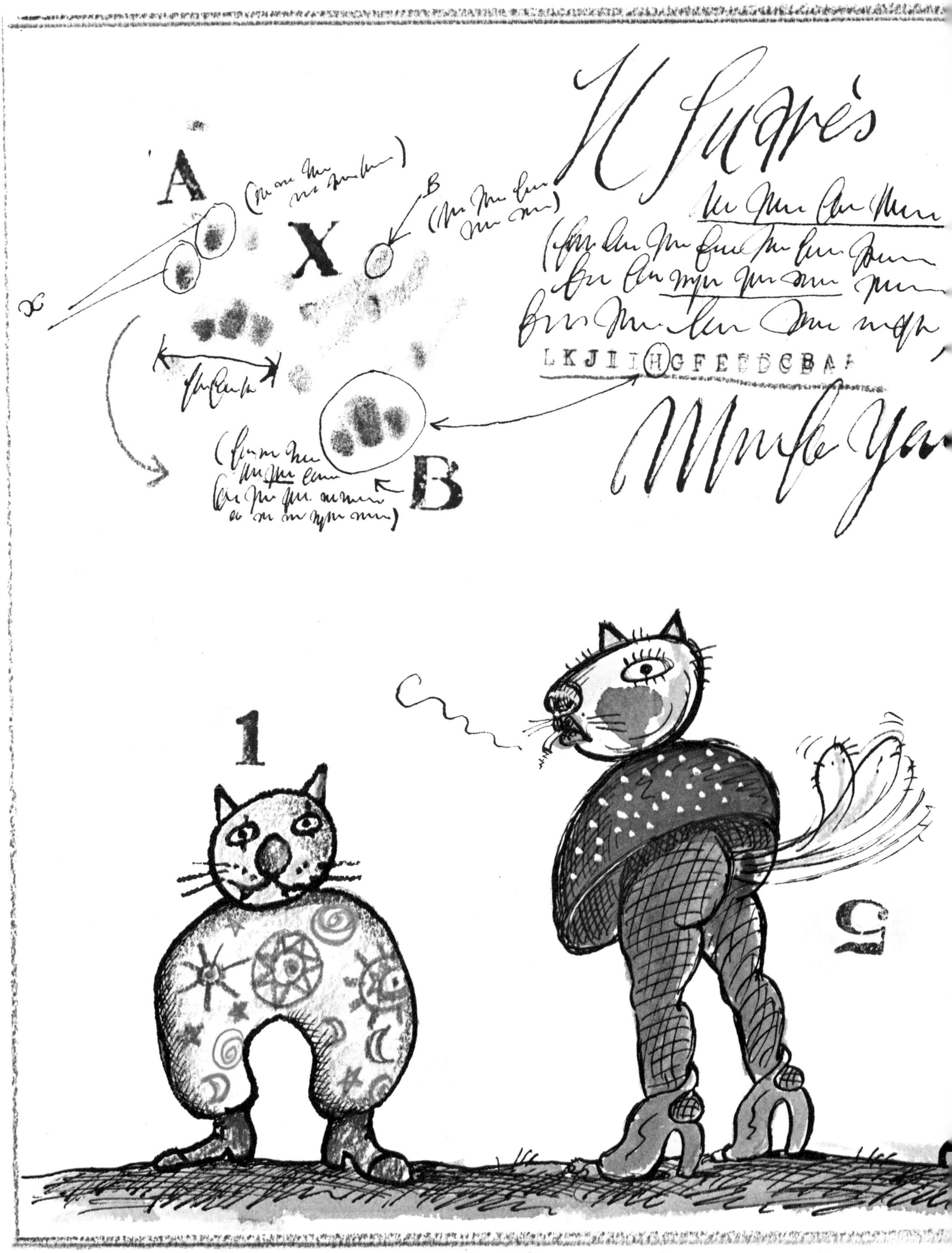
A
X
B
LKJIIHGFEDCBA
B
1

Mark Twain

1835-1910

THE KITTEN
IN THE
CORNER-POCKET

Redding, Connecticut,
Oct. 2, 08.

Dear Mrs. Patterson,—The contents of your letter are very pleasant and very welcome, and I thank you for them, sincerely. If I can find a photograph of my "Tammany" and her kittens, I will enclose it in this. One of them likes to be crammed into a corner-pocket of the billiard table—which he fits as snugly as does a finger in a glove and then he watches the game (and obstructs it) by the hour, and spoils many a shot by putting out his paw and changing the direction of a passing ball. Whenever a ball is in his arms, or so close to him that it cannot be played upon without risk of hurting him, the player is privileged to remove it to anyone of the 3 spots that chances to be vacant. . . .

Sincerely yours,
S. L. Clemens.

DICK BAKER'S
CAT

One of my comrades there—another of those victims of eighteen years of unrequited toil and blighted hopes—was one of the gentlest spirits that ever bore its patient cross in a weary exile; grave and simple Dick Baker, pocket-miner of Dead-Horse Gulch. He was forty-six, grey as a rat, earnest, thoughtful, slenderly educated, slouchily dressed and clay-soiled, but his heart was finer metal than any gold his shovel ever brought to light—than any, indeed, that ever was mined or minted.

Whenever he was out of luck and a little downhearted, he would fall to mourning over the loss of a wonderful cat he used to own (for where women and children are not, men of kindly impulses take up with pets, for they must love something). And he always spoke of the strange sagacity of that cat with the air of a man who believed in his secret heart that there was something human about it— maybe even supernatural.

I heard him talking about this animal once. He said: 'Gentlemen, I used to have a cat here, by the name of Tom Quartz, which you'd 'a' took an interest in, I reckon—most anybody would. I had him here eight year—and he was the remarkablest cat *I* ever see. He was a large grey one of the Tom specie, an' he had more hard, natchral sense than any man in this camp—'n' a *power* of dignity—he wouldn't let the Gov'ner of Californy be familiar with him. He never ketched a rat in his life—'peared to be above it. He never cared for nothing but mining. He knowed more about mining, that cat did, than any man *I* ever, ever see. You couldn't tell *him* noth'n' 'bout placer-diggin's—'n' as for pocket-mining, why he was just born for it. He would dig out after me an' Jim when we went over the hills prospect'n', and he would trot along behind us for as much as five mile, if we went so fur. An' he had the best judgement about mining-ground —why, you never see anything like it. When we went to work, he'd scatter a glance round, 'n' if he didn't think much of the indications, he would give a look as much as to say, "Well, I'll have to get you to excuse *me*"—'n' without another word he'd hyste his nose in the air 'n' shove for home. But if the ground suited him, he would lay low 'n' keep dark till the first pan was washed, 'n' then he would sidle up 'n' take a look, an' if there was about six or seven grains of gold *he* was satisfied—he didn't want no better prospect 'n' that—'n' then he would law down on our coats and snore like a steamboat till we'd struck the pocket, an' then get up 'n' superintend. He was nearly lightnin' on superintending.

'Well, by an' by, up comes this yer quartz excitement. Everybody was into it—everybody was pick'n' 'n' blast'n' instead of shovellin' dirt on the hillside—everybody was putt'n' down a shaft instead of scrapin' the surface. Noth'n' would do Jim, but *we* must tackle the ledges, too, 'n' so we did. We commenced putt'n' down a shaft, 'n' Tom Quartz he begin to wonder what in the dickens it was all about. *He* hadn't ever seen any mining like that before, 'n' he was all upset, as you may say— he couldn't come to a right understanding of it no way—it was too many for *him*. He was down on it too, you bet you—he was down on it powerful—'n' always appeared to consider it the cussedest foolishness out. But that cat, you know, was *always* agin' new-fangled arrangements—somehow he never could abide 'em. *You* know how it is with old habits. But by and by Tom Quartz begin to git sort of reconciled a little though he never *could* altogether understand that eternal sinkin' of a shaft an' never

104

pannin' out anything. At last he got to comin' down in the shaft, hisself, to try to cipher it out. An' when he'd git the blues, 'n' feel kind o' scruffy, 'n' aggravated 'n' disgusted—knowin' as he did, that the bills was runnin' up all the time an' we warn't makin' a cent—he would curl up on a gunny-sack in the corner an' go to sleep. Well, one day when the shaft was down about eight foot, the rock got so hard that we had to put in a blast—the first blast 'n' we'd ever done since Tom Quartz was born. An' then we lit the fuse 'n' clumb out 'n' got off 'bout fifty yards—'n' forgot 'n' left Tom Quartz sound asleep on the gunny-sack. In 'bout a minute we seen a puff of smoke bust up out of the hole, 'n' then everything let go with an awful crash, 'n' about four million ton of rocks 'n' dirt 'n' smoke 'n' splinters shot up 'bout a mile an' a half into the air, an' by George, right in the dead centre of it was old Tom Quartz a-goin' end over end, an' a-snortin' an' a-sneezin', an' a-clawin' an' a-reach'n' for things like all possessed. But it warn't no use, you know, it warn't no use. An' that was the last we see of *him* for about two minutes 'n' a half, an' then all of a sudden it began to rain rocks and rubbage an' directly he come down ker-whoop about ten foot off f'm where we stood. Well, I reckon he was p'raps the orneriest-lookin' beast you ever see. One ear was sot back on his neck, 'n' his tail was stove up, 'n' his eye-winkers was singed off, 'n' he was all

blacked up with powder an' smoke, an' all sloppy with mud 'n' slush f'm one end to the other. Well, sir, it warn't no use to try to apologize—we couldn't say a word. He took a sort of disgusted look at himself, 'n' then he looked at us—an' it was just exactly the same as if he had said—"Gents, maybe *you* think it's smart to take advantage of a cat that ain't had no experience of quartz-minin', but *I* think different"—an' then he turned on his heel 'n' marched off home without ever saying another word.

'That was jest his style. An' maybe you won't believe it, but after that you never see a cat so prejudiced agin' quartz-mining as what he was. An' by an' by when he *did* get to goin' down in the shaft agin', you'd 'a' been astonished at his sagacity. The minute we'd tetch off a blast 'n' the fuse'd begin to sizzle, he'd give a look as much as to say, "Well, I'll have to git you to excuse *me*," an' it was surpris'n' the way he'd shin out of that hole 'n' go f'r a tree. Sagacity? It ain't no name for it. 'Twas inspiration!'

I said, 'Well, Mr Baker, his prejudice against quartz-mining *was* remarkable, considering how he came by it. Couldn't you ever cure him of it?'

'*Cure him!* No! When Tom Quartz was sot once, he was *always* sot—and you might 'a' blowed him up as much as three million times 'n' you'd never 'a' broken him of his cussed prejudice agin' quartz-mining.'

AT THE ZOO

In the great Zoological Gardens [of Marseille] we found specimens of all the animals the world produces, I think...The boon companion of the colossal elephant was a common cat! This cat had a fashion of climbing up the elephant's hind legs, and roosting on his back. She would sit up there, with her paws curved under her breast, and sleep in the sun half the afternoon. It used to annoy the elephant at first and he would reach up and take her down, but she would go aft and climb up again. She persisted until she finally conquered the elephant's prejudices, and now they are inseparable friends. The cat plays about her comrade's forefeet or his trunk often, until dogs approach, and then she goes aloft out of danger. The elephant has annihilated several dogs lately, that pressed his companion too closely.

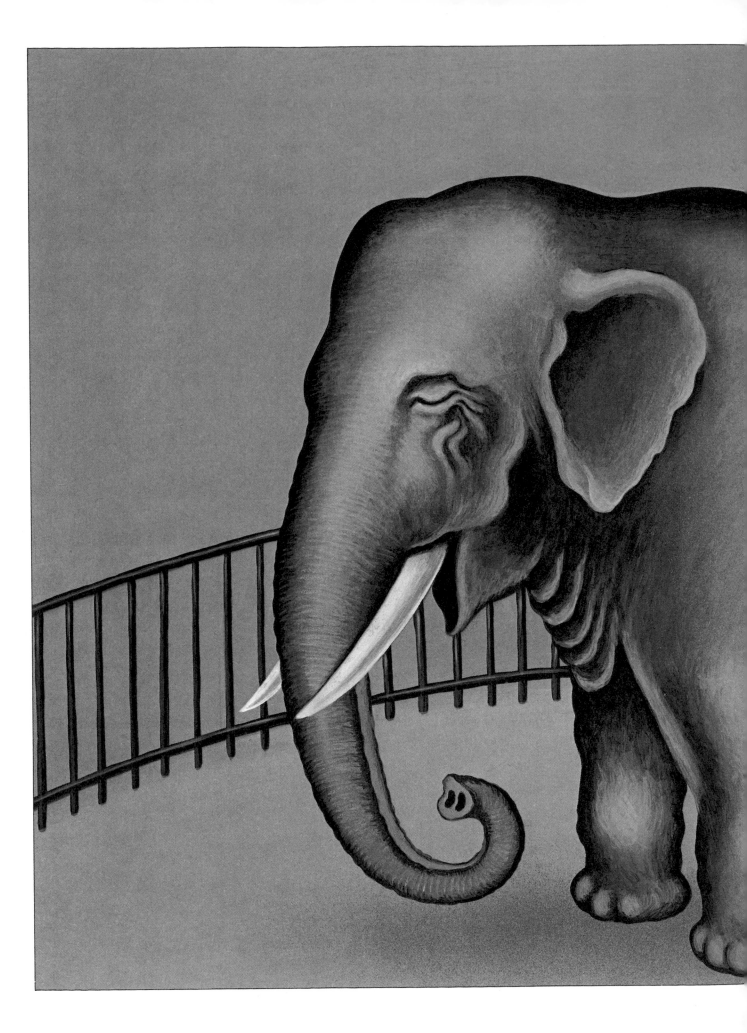

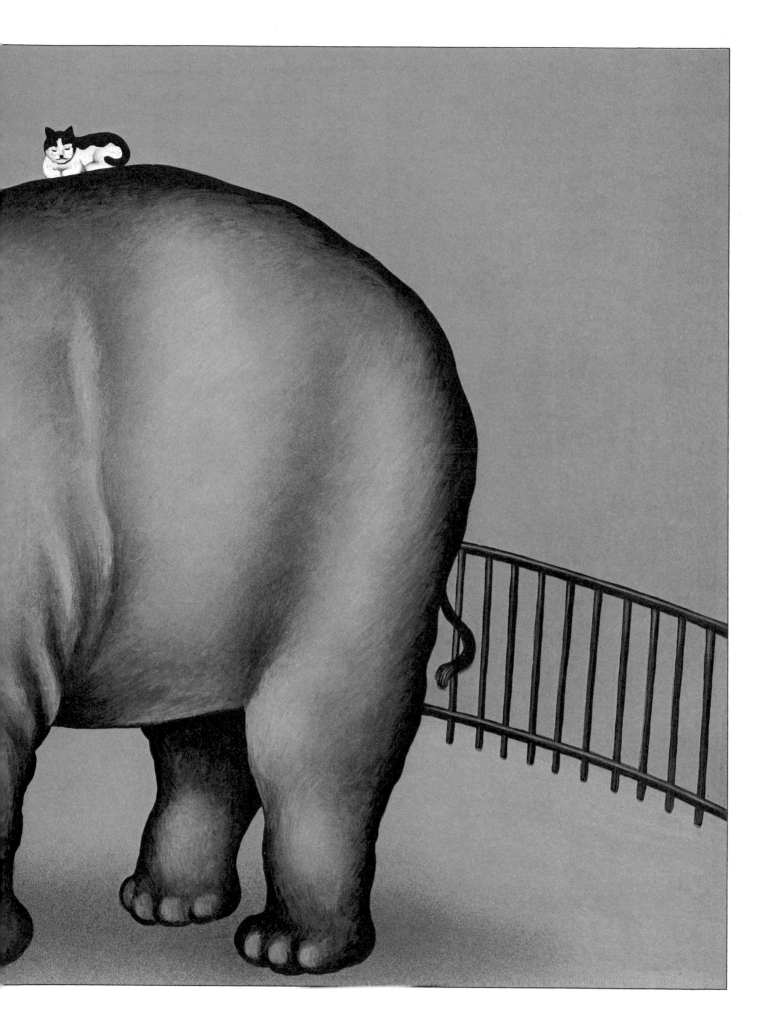

Sir Richard Burton

1821-1890

A TALE OF
THE CAT
AND THE CROW

Once upon a time, a crow and a cat lived in brotherhood; and one day as they were together under a tree, behold, they spied a leopard making towards them, and they were not aware of his approach till he was close upon them. The crow at once flew up to the tree-top; but the cat abode confounded and said to the crow, "O my friend, hast thou no device to save me, even as all my hope is in thee?" Replied the crow, "Of very truth it behoveth brethren, in case of need, to cast about for a device when peril overtaketh them, and how well saith the poet,

> A friend in need is he who, ever true,
> For thy well-doing would himself undo:
> One who when Fortune gars us parting rue
> Victimeth self reunion to renew."

Now hard by that tree were shepherds with their dogs; so the crow flew towards them and smote the face of the earth with his wings, cawing and crying out. Furthermore he went up to one of the dogs and flapped his wings in his face and flew up a little way, whilst the dog ran after him thinking to catch him. Presently, one of the shepherds raised his head and saw the bird flying near the ground and lighting alternately so he followed him, and the crow ceased not flying just high enough to save himself and to throw out the dogs; and yet tempting them to follow for the purpose of tearing him to pieces. But as soon as they came near him, he would fly up a little; and so at last he brought them to the tree, under which was the leopard. And when the dogs saw him they rushed upon him and he turned and fled. Now the leopard thought to eat the cat who was saved by the craft of his friend the crow.

Translation from A Thousand and One Nights

A lame cat is better than a swift horse when rats infest the palace.   *Chinese Proverb*

108

Christopher Smart

1722-1771

CAT
JEOFFRY

For I will consider my Cat Jeoffry.
For he is the servant of the Living God, duly and
    daily serving him.
For at the first glance of the glory of God in the East
    he worships in his way.
For this is done by wreathing his body seven times
    round with elegant quickness.
For then he leaps up to catch the musk, which is the
    blessing of God upon his prayer.
For he rolls upon prank to work it in.
For having done duty and received blessing he
    begins to consider himself.
For this he performs in ten degrees.
For first he looks upon his fore-paws to see if they
    are clean.

For secondly he kicks up behind to clear away
there.

For thirdly he works it upon stretch with the fore-
paws extended.

For fourthly he sharpens his paws with wood.

For fifthly he washes himself.

For sixthly he rolls upon wash.

For seventhly he fleas himself, that he may not be
interrupted upon the beat.

For eighthly he rubs himself against a post.

For ninthly he looks up for his instructions.

For tenthly he goes in quest of food.

For having consider'd God and himself he will
consider his neighbour.

For if he meets another cat he will kiss her in
kindness.

For when he takes his prey he plays with it to give
it a chance.

For one mouse in seven escapes by his dallying.

For when his day's work is done his business more
properly begins.

For he keeps the Lord's watch in the night against
the adversary.

For he counteracts the powers of darkness by his
electrical skin and glaring eyes.

For he counteracts the Devil, who is death, by
brisking about the life.

For in the morning orisons he loves the sun and the
sun loves him.

For he is of the tribe of Tiger.

For the Cherub Cat is a term of the Angel Tiger.

For he has the subtlety and hissing of a serpent,
which in goodness he suppresses.

For he will not do destruction, if he is well-fed,
neither will he spit without provocation.

For he purrs in thankfulness, when God tells him
he's a good Cat.

For he is an instrument for the children to learn
benevolence upon.

For every house is incompleat without him and a
blessing is lacking in the spirit.

For the Lord commanded Moses concerning the
cats at the departure of the Children of Israel
from Egypt.

For every family had one cat at least in the bag.

For the English Cats are the best in Europe.

For he is the cleanest in the use of his forepaws of
any quadrupede.

For the dexterity of his defense is an instance of the
love of God to him exceedingly.

For he is the quickest to his mark of any creature.

For he is tenacious of his point.

For he is a mixture of gravity and waggery.

For he knows that God is his Saviour.

For there is nothing sweeter than his peace when at
rest.

For there is nothing brisker than his life when in
motion.

For he is of the Lord's poor, and so indeed is he
called by benevolence perpetually—Poor
Jeoffry! poor Jeoffry! the rat has bit thy throat.

For I bless the name of the Lord Jesus that Jeoffry
is better.

For the divine spirit comes about his body to sustain
it in compleat cat.

For his tongue is exceeding pure so that it has in
purity what it wants in musick.

For he is docile and can learn certain things.

For he can set up with gravity which is patience
upon approbation.

For he can fetch and carry, which is patience in
employment.

For he can jump over a stick which is patience upon
proof positive.

For he can spraggle upon waggle at the word of
command.

For he can jump from an eminence into his
master's bosom.

For he can catch the cork and toss it again.

For he is hated by the hypocrite and miser.

For the former is afraid of detection.

For the latter refuses the charge.

For he camels his back to bear the first motion of
business.

For he is good to think on, if a man would express
himself neatly.

For he made a great figure in Egypt for his signal
services.

For he killed the Icneumon-rat very pernicious by
land.

For his ears are so acute that they sting again.

For from this proceeds the passing quickness of his
attention.

For by stroking of him I have found out electricity.

For I perceived God's light about him both wax and
fire.

For the electrical fire is the spiritual substance,
which God sends from heaven to sustain the
bodies both of man and beast.

For God has blessed him in the variety of his
movements.

For, tho' he cannot fly, he is an excellent clamberer.

For his motions upon the face of the earth are more
than any other quadrupede.

For he can tread to all the measures upon the
musick.

For he can swim for life.

For he can creep.

For in his
morning Orisons
he loves the Sun
and the Sun
loves him
for he is of the
tribe of Tiger.

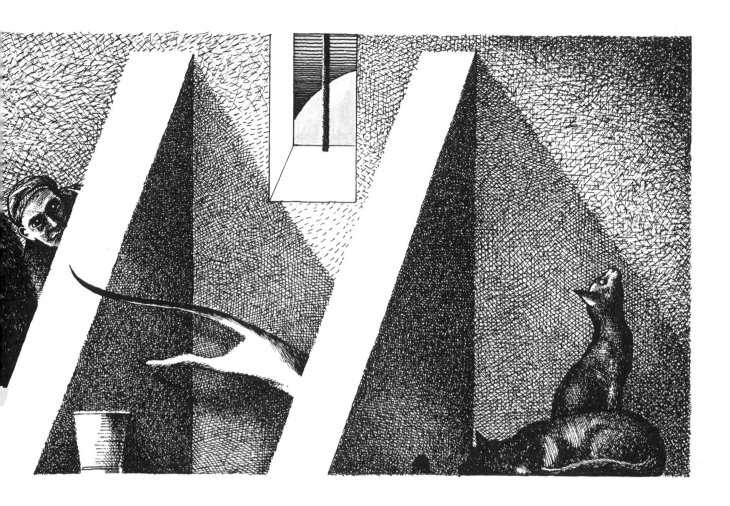

Walter de la Mare

1873-1956

BROOMSTICKS

Miss Chauncey's cat, Sam, had been with her many years before she noticed anything unusual, anything *disturbing,* in his conduct. Like most cats who live under the same roof with but one or two humans, he had always been more sagacious than cats of a common household. He had learned Miss Chauncey's ways. He acted, that is, as nearly like a small mortal dressed up in a hairy coat as one could expect a cat to act. He was what is called an "intelligent" cat.

But though Sam had learned much from Miss Chauncey, I am bound to say that Miss Chauncey had learned very little from Sam. She was a kind indulgent mistress; she could sew, and cook, and crochet, and make a bed, and read and write and cipher a little. And when she was a girl she used to sing "Kathleen Mavourneen" to the piano. Sam, of course, could do nothing of this kind.

But then, Miss Chauncey could no more have caught and killed a mouse or a blackbird with her five naked fingers than she could have been Pope of Rome. Nor could she run up a six-foot brick wall, or leap clean from the hearth-mat in her parlour on to the shelf of her chimney-piece without disturbing a single ornament, or even tinkle one crystal glass-drop against another. Unlike Sam, she could not find her way in the dark, or by her sense of smell; or keep in good health by merely nibbling grass in the garden. If, moreover, as a little girl she had been held up by her feet and hands two or three feet above the ground and then dropped, she would have at once fallen plump on her back, whereas when Sam was only a three-month-old, he could have managed to twist clean about in the air in twelve inches and come down on his four feet as firm as a table.

While Sam, then, had learned a good deal from Miss Chauncey, she had learned nothing from him.

And even if she had been willing to be taught, it is doubtful if she would ever have proved even a promising pupil. What is more, she knew much less about Sam than he knew about his mistress—until, at least, that afternoon when she was doing her hair in the glass. And then she could hardly believe her own eyes. It was a moment that completely changed her views about Sam—and nothing after that experience was ever quite the same again.

Sam had always been a fine upstanding creature, his fur jet-black and silky, his eyes a lambent green, even in sunshine, and at night a-glow like green topazes. He was now full seven years of age, and had an unusually powerful miaou. Living as he did quite alone with Miss Chauncey at Post Houses, it was natural that he should become her constant companion. For Post Houses was a singularly solitary house, standing almost in the middle of Haggurdsdon Moor, just where two wandering byways cross each other like the half-closed blades of a pair of shears or scissors.

It was a mile and a half from its nearest neighbour, Mr. Cullings, the carrier; and yet another quarter of a mile from the village of Haggurdsdon. Its roads were extremely ancient. They had been sheep-tracks long before the Romans came to England and had cut *their* roads from shore to shore. But for many years past few travellers or carts or even sheep with their shepherd came Miss Chauncey's way. You could have gazed from her windows for hours together, even on a summer's day, without seeing so much as a tinker's barrow or a gipsy's van.

Post Houses, too, was perhaps the ugliest house there ever was. Its four corners stood straight up on the moor like a house of nursery bricks. From its flat roof on a clear day the eye could see for miles across the moor, Mr. Cullings' cottage being out of sight in a shallow hollow. It had belonged to Miss Chauncey's ancestors for numbers of generations. Many people in Haggurdsdon indeed called it Chauncey's. And though in a great wind it was almost as full of noises as an organ, though it was a cold barn in winter and though another branch of the family had as far back as the seventies gone to live in the Isle of Wight, Miss Chauncey still remained faithful to its four walls. In fact she loved the ugly old place, for she had lived in it ever since she was a little girl with knickerbockers showing under her skirts and pale-blue ribbon shoulder knots.

This fact alone made Sam's conduct the more reprehensible, for never cat had kinder mistress. Miss Chauncey herself was now about sixty years of age—fifty-three years older than Sam. She was five foot ten-and-a-half inches in height. On weekdays she wore black alpaca, and on Sundays a watered silk. Her large round steel spectacles straddling across her high nose gave her a look of being keen as well as cold. But truly she was neither. For even so stupid a man as Mr. Cullings could take her in over the cartage charge of a parcel—just by looking tired or sighing as he glanced at his rough-haired, knock-kneed mare. And there was the warmest of hearts under her stiff bodice.

Being so far from the village, milk and cream were a little difficult, of course. But Miss Chauncey could deny Sam nothing—in reason. She paid a whole sixpence a week to a little girl called Susan Ard who brought these dainties from the nearest farm. They were dainties indeed, for though the grasses on Haggurdsdon Moor were of dark sour green, the cows that grazed on it gave an uncommonly rich milk, and Sam flourished on it. Mr. Cullings called once a week on his round, and had a standing order to bring with him a few sprats or fresh herrings, or any other toothsome fish that was in season. Miss Chauncey would not even withold her purse from expensive whitebait, if no other cheaper fish were procurable. And Mr. Cullings would eye Sam fawning about his cartwheel, or gloating up at his dish, and say, "'Ee be a queer animal, shure enough; 'ee be a wunnerful queer animal, 'ee be."

As for Miss Chauncey herself, she was a niggardly eater, though much attached to her tea. She made her own bread and biscuits. On Saturday a butcher-boy drove up in a striped apron. Besides which she was a wonderful manager. Her cupboards were full of homemade jams and bottled fruits and dried herbs—everything of that kind, for Post Houses had a nice long strip of garden behind it, surrounded by a high old yellow brick wall.

Quite early in life Sam, of course, had learned to know his mealtime—though how he "told" it was known only to himself, for he never appeared to glance at the face of the grandfather's clock on the staircase. He was punctual, particularly in his toilet, and a prodigious sleeper. He had learned to pull down the latch of the back door, if, in the months when an open window was not to be found, he wished to go out. Indeed at last he preferred the latch. He never slept on Miss Chauncey's patchwork quilt, unless his own had been placed over it. He was particular almost to a foppish degree in his habits, and he was no thief. He had a mew on one note to show when he wanted something to eat; a mew a semitone or two higher if he wanted drink (that is, cold water, for which he had a great taste); and yet another mew—gentle and sustained—when he wished, so to speak, to converse with his mistress.

Not, of course, that the creature talked *English*, but he liked to sit up on one chair by the fireside, especially in the kitchen—for he was no born parlour-cat—and to look up at the glinting glasses of Miss Chauncey's spectacles, and then down awhile at the fire-flames (drawing his claws in and out as he did so, and purring the while), almost as if he might be preaching a sermon, or reciting a poem.

But this was in the happy days when all seemed well. This was in the days when Miss Chauncey's mind was innocent of all doubts and suspicions. Like others of his kind, too, Sam delighted to lie in the window and idly watch the birds in the apple-trees—tits and bullfinches and dunnocks—or to crouch over a mouse-hole for hours together. Such were his amusements (for he never ate his mice) while Miss Chauncey with cap and broom, duster and dishclout, went about her housework. But he also had a way of examining things in which cats are not generally interested. He as good as told Miss Chauncey one afternoon that a hole was coming in her parlour carpet. For he walked to and fro and back and forth with his tail up, until she attended to him. And he certainly warned her, with a yelp like an Amazonian monkey, when a red-hot coal had set her kitchen mat on fire.

He would lie or sit with his whiskers to the North before noonday, and due South afterwards. In general his manners were perfection. But occasionally when she called him, his face would appear to knot itself into a frown—at any rate to assume a low sullen look, as if he expostulated "Why must you be interrupting me, Madam, when I am thinking of something else?" And now and then, Miss Chauncey fancied he would deliberately secrete himself or steal out and in of Post Houses unbeknown.

Miss Chauncey, too, would sometimes find him trotting from room to room as if on a visit of inspection. On his fifth birthday he had brought an immense mouse and laid it beside the patent toe-cap of her boot, as she sat knitting by the fire. She smiled and nodded merrily at him, as usual, but on this occasion he had looked at her intently, and then deliberately shook his head. After that, he never paid the smallest attention to mouse or mouse-hole or mousery, and Miss Chauncey was obliged to purchase a cheese-bait trap, else she would have been overrun.

Almost any domestic cat may do things of this nature, and of course all this was solely on Sam's domestic side. For he shared a house with Miss

113

Chauncey and, like any two beings that live together, he was bound to keep up certain appearances. He met her half-way, as the saying goes. When, however, he was "on his own", he was no longer Miss Chauncey's Sam, he was no longer merely the cat at Post Houses, but just *himself*. He went back, that is, to his own free independent life; to his own private habits.

Then the moor on which he roved was his own country, and the humans and their houses on it were no more to him in his wild, privy existence than molehills or badgers' earths, or rabbits' mounds, are to us. On this side of his life his mistress knew practically nothing. She did not consider it. She supposed that Sam behaved like other cats, though it was evident that at times he went far abroad, for he now and then brought home a Cochin China chick, and the nearest Cochin China fowls were at the vicarage, a good four miles off. Sometimes of an evening, too, when Miss Chauncey was taking a little walk herself, she would see him—a swiftly-moving black speck—far along the road, hastening home. And there was more purpose expressed in his gait and appearance than ever Mr. Cullings showed!

It was pleasant to observe, too, when he came within miaouing distance how his manner changed. He turned at once from being a Cat into being a Domestic Cat. He was instantaneously no longer the Feline Adventurer, the Nocturnal Marauder and Haunter of Haggurdsdon Moor (though Miss Chauncey would not have so expressed it), but simply his mistress' spoiled pet, Sam. She loved him dearly. But, as again with human beings who are accustomed to live together, she did not *think* very much about him. It could not but be a shock then that latish afternoon, when without the slightest warning Miss Chauncey discovered that Sam was deliberately deceiving her!

She was brushing her thin brown front hair before her looking-glass. And this moment it hung down over her face like a fine loose veil. And as she always mused of other things when she was brushing her hair, she was somewhat absentminded the while. Then suddenly on raising her eyes behind this mesh of hair, she perceived not only that Sam's reflection was in sight of the looking-glass, but that something a little mysterious was happening. Sam was sitting up as if to beg. There was nothing in that. It had been a customary feat of his since he was six months old. Still, for what might he be begging, no one by?

Now the window to the right of the chintz-valanced dressing-table was open at the top. Without,

it was beginning to grow dark. All Haggurdsdon Moor lay hushed and still in the evening's coming gloom. And apart from begging when there was nothing to beg for, Sam seemed, so to speak, to be gesticulating with his paws. He appeared, that is, to be making signs, just as if there were someone or something looking in at the window at him from out of the air—which was quite impossible. And there was a look upon his face that certainly Miss Chauncey had never seen before.

She stayed a moment with her hair-brush uplifted, her long lean arm at an angle with her head. On seeing this, Sam had instantly desisted from these motions. He had dropped to his fours again, and was now apparently composing himself for another nap. No; this too was a pretence, for presently as she watched, he turned restlessly about so that his whiskers were once again due South. His backward part toward the window, he was now gazing straight in front of him out of a far from friendly face. Far indeed from friendly for a creature that has lived with you ever since he opened the eyes of his first kittenhood.

As if he had read her thoughts, Sam at that moment lifted his head to look at his mistress; she withdrew her eyes to the glass only in the nick of time and when she turned from her toilet there sat he—so serene in appearance, so puss-like, so ordinary once more that Miss Chauncey could scarcely believe anything whatever had been amiss. Had her eyes deluded her—her glass? Was that peculiar motion of Sam's fore-paws (almost as if he were knitting), was that wide excited stare only due to the fact that he was catching what was, to her, an invisible fly?

Miss Chauncey having now neatly arranged her "window-curtains"—the sleek loops of hair she wore on either side her high forehead—glanced yet again at the window. Nothing there but the silence of the moor; nothing there but the faint pricking of a star as the evening darkened.

Sam's cream was waiting on the hearthrug in the parlour as usual at five o'clock. The lamp was lit. The red blinds were drawn. The fire crackled in the grate. There they sat, these two; the walls of the four-cornered house beside the crossroads rising up above them like a huge oblong box under the immense starry sky that saucered in the wide darkness of the moor.

And while she so sat—with Sam there, seemingly fast asleep—Miss Chauncey was thinking. What had occurred in the bedroom that early evening had reminded her of other odd little bygone happenings. Trifles she had scarcely noticed but which now returned clearly to memory. How often in the past, for example, Sam at this hour would be sitting as if fast asleep (as now) his paws tucked neatly in, looking much like a stout alderman after a high dinner. And then suddenly, without warning, as if a distant voice had called him, he would leap to his feet and run straight out of the room. And somewhere in the house—door ajar or window agape, he would find his egress and be up and away into the night. This had been a common thing to happen.

Once, too, Miss Chauncey had found him squatting on his hind-quarters on the window-ledge of a little room that had been entirely disused since her fair little Cousin Milly had stayed at Post Houses when Miss Chauncey was a child of eight. She had cried out at sight of him, "You foolish Sam, you! Come in, sir. You will be tumbling out of the window next!" And she remembered as if it were yesterday that though at this he had stepped gingerly in at once from his dizzy perch, he had not looked at her. He had passed her without a sign.

On moonlight evenings, too—why, you could never be sure where he was. You could never be sure from what errand he had *returned*. Was she sure indeed where he was on *any* night? The longer she reflected, the deeper grew her doubts and misgivings. This night, at any rate, Miss Chauncey determined to keep watch. But she was not happy in doing so. She hated all manner of spying. They were old companions, Sam and she; and she, without him, in bleak Post Houses, would be sadly desolate. She loved Sam dearly. None the less, the spectacle of that afternoon haunted her, and it would be wiser to know all that there was to be known, even if for Sam's sake only.

Now Miss Chauncey always slept with her bedroom door ajar. She had slept so ever since her nursery days. Being a rather timid little girl, she liked in those far-away times to hear the grown-up voices downstairs and the spoons and forks clinking. As for Sam, he always slept in his basket beside her fireplace. Every morning there he would be, though on some mornings Miss Chauncey's eyes would open gently to find herself gazing steadily into his pale-green ones as he stood on his hind-paws, resting his front ones on her bed-side, and looking up into her face. "Time for your milk, Sam?" his mistress would murmur. And Sam would mew, as distantly almost as a seagull in the height of the sky.

Tonight, however, Miss Chauncey only pretended to fall asleep. It was difficult, however, to keep wholly awake, and she was all but drowsing off when there came a faint squeak from the hinge of her door, and she realised that Sam was gone out. After waiting a moment or two, she struck a match. Yes, there was his empty basket in the dark silent room, and presently from far away—from the steeple at Haggurdson Village—came the knolling of midnight.

Miss Chauncey placed the dead end of the match in the saucer of her candlestick, and at that moment fancied she heard a faint *whssh* at her window, as of a sudden gust or scurry of wind, or the wings of a fast-flying bird—of a wild goose. It even reminded Miss Chauncey of half-forgotten Guy Fawkes Days and of the sound the stick of a rocket makes as it sweeps down through the air while its green and ruby lights die out in the immense heavens above. Miss Chauncey gathered up her long legs in the bed, drew on the flannel dressing-gown that always hung on her bed-rail, and lifting back the blind an inch or two, looked out of the window.

It was a high starry night, and a brightening in the sky above the roof seemed to betoken there must be a moon over the backward parts of the house. Even as she watched, a streak of pale silver descended swiftly out of the far spaces of the heavens where a few large stars were gathered as if in the shape of a sickle. It was a meteorite; and at that very instant Miss Chauncey fancied she heard a faint remote dwindling *whssh* in the air. Was *that* a meteor too? Could she have been deceived? Was she being deceived in everything? She drew back.

And then, as if in deliberate and defiant answer, out of the distance, from what appeared to be the extreme end of her long garden, where grew a tangle of sloe bushes, there followed a prolonged and as if half-secret caterwaul; very low—contralto, one might say—*Meearou-rou-rou-rou-rou*.

Heaven forbid! Was *that* Sam's tongue? The caterwauling ceased. Yet still Miss Chauncey could not suppress a shudder. She knew Sam's voice of old. But surely not that! Surely not that!

Strange and immodest, too, though it was to hear herself in that solitary place calling out in the dead of night, she none the less at once opened the window and summoned Sam by name. There was no response. The trees and bushes of the garden stood motionless; their faint shadows on the ground revealing how small a moon was actually in the sky, and how low it hung towards its setting. The vague undulations of the moor stretched into the distance. Not a light to be seen except those of the firmament. Again, and yet again, Miss Chauncey cried, "Sam, Sam! Come away in! Come away in, sir, you bad creature!" Not a sound. Not the least stir of leaf or blade of grass.

When, after so broken a night, Miss Chauncey awoke a little late the next morning, the first thing her eyes beheld when she sat up in bed was Sam—couched as usual in his basket. It was a mystery, an uneasy one. After supping up his morning bowl, he slept steadily on until noonday. This happened to be the day of the week when Miss Chauncey made bread. On and on she steadily kneaded the dough with her knuckled hands, glancing ever and again towards the motionless creature. With fingers clotted from the great earthenware bowl, she stood over him at last for a few moments, and looked at him closely.

He was lying curled round with his whiskered face to one side towards the fire. And it seemed to Miss Chauncey that she had never noticed before that faint peculiar grin on his face. "Sam!" she cried sharply. An eye instantly opened, fiercely green as if a mouse had squeaked. He stared at her for an instant; then the lid narrowed. The gaze slunk away a little, but Sam began to purr.

The truth of it is, all this was making Miss Chauncey exceedingly unhappy. Mr. Cullings called that afternoon with a basket of some fine comely young sprats. "Them'll wake his Royal Highness up," he said. "They'm fresh as daisies. Lor, m'm, what a Nero that beast be!"

"Cats *are* strange creatures, Mr. Cullings," replied Miss Chauncey reflectively, complacently, supposing that Mr. Cullings had misplaced an *h* and had meant to say *an hero*. And Sam himself, with uplifted tail, and as if of the same opinion, was rubbing his head gently against her boot.

Mr. Cullings eyed her closely. 'Why, yes, they be," he said. "What I say is, is that as soon as they're out of sight, you are out of their mind. There's no more gratitood nor affection in a cat than in a pump. Though so far as the pump is concerned, the gratitood should be on our side. I knew a Family of Cats once what fairly druv their mistress out of house and home."

"But you wouldn't have a cat *only* a pet?" said Miss Chauncey faintly; afraid to ask for further particulars of the peculiar occurrence.

"Why no, m'm," said the carrier. "As the Lord made 'em, so they be. But I'll be bound they could tell some knotty stories if they had a human tongue in their heads!"

Sam had ceased caressing his mistress's foot, and was looking steadily at Mr. Cullings, his hair roughed a little about the neck and shoulders. And the carrier looked back.

"No, m'm. We wouldn't keep 'em," he said at last "if they was *four* times that size. Or, not for long!"

Having watched Mr. Cullings' little cart bowl away into the distance, Miss Chauncey returned into the house, more disturbed than ever. Nor did her uneasiness abate when Sam refused even to sniff at his sprats. Instead, he crawled under a low table in the kitchen, behind the old seaman's chest in which Miss Chauncey kept her kindling-wood. She fancied she heard his claws working in the wood now and again; once he seemed to be expressing his natural feelings in what vulgar people with little sympathy for anmials describe as "swearing".

Her caressing "Sams", at any rate, were all in vain. His only reply was a kind of sneeze which uncomfortably resembled "spitting". Miss Chauncey's feelings had already been hurt. It was now her mind that suffered. Something the carrier had said, or the way he had said it, or the peculiar look she had noticed on his face when he was returning Sam's stare in the porch, haunted her thoughts. She was no longer young; was she becoming fanciful? Or must she indeed conclude that for weeks past Sam had been steadily deceiving her, or at any rate concealing his wanderings and his interests? What nonsense! Worse still:—Was she now so credulous as to believe that Sam had in actual fact been making signals—and secretly, behind her back—to some confederate that must either have been up in the sky, or in the moon!

Whether or not, Miss Chauncey determined to keep a sharper eye on him, if for his own sake only. She would at least make sure that he did not leave the house that night. But then: why not? she asked herself. Why shouldn't the creature choose his own hour and season? Cats, like owls, *see* best in the dark. They go best a-mousing in the dark, and may prefer the dark for their private, social, and even public affairs. Post Houses, after all, was only rather more than two miles from Haggurdsdon Village, and there were cats there in plenty. Poor fellow, her own dumb human company must sometimes be dull enough!

Such were Miss Chauncey's reflections; and as if to reassure her, Sam himself at that moment serenely entered the room and leaped up on to the empty chair beside her tea-table. As if, too, to prove that he had thought better of his evil temper, or to insinuate that there had been nothing amiss between himself and Mr. Cullings, he was licking his chops, and there was no mistaking the odour of fish which he brought in with him from his saucer.

"So you have thought better of it, my boy?" thought Miss Chauncey, though she did not utter the words aloud. And yet as she returned his steady feline gaze, she realised how difficult it was to read

the intelligence behind those eyes. You might say that, Sam being only a cat, there was no meaning in them at all. But Miss Chauncey knew she couldn't have said it if such eyes had looked out of a *human* shape at her! She would have been acutely alarmed.

Unfortunately, and almost as if Sam had overheard his mistress' speculations regarding possible cat friends in the Village, there came at that moment a faint ambling mew beneath the open window. In a flash Sam was out of his chair and over the window ledge, and Miss Chauncey rose only just in time to see him in infuriated pursuit of a slim sleek tortoiseshell creature that had evidently come to Post Houses in hope of a friendlier reception, and was now fleeing in positive fear of its life.

Sam returned from his chase as fresh as paint, and Miss Chauncey was horrified to detect—caught up between the claws of his right foot—a tuft or two of tortoiseshell fur, which, having composed himself by the fire, he promptly removed by licking.

Still pondering on these disquieting events, Miss Chauncey took her usual evening walk in the garden. Candytuft and Virginia stock were blossoming along the shell-lined path, and roses were already beginning to blow on the high brick wall which shut off her narrow strip of land from the vast lap of the moor. Having come to the end of the path, Miss Chauncey pushed on a little farther than usual, to where the grasses grew more rampant, and where wild headlong weeds raised their heads beneath her few lichenous apple trees. Still farther down—for hers was a long, though narrow, garden—there grew straggling bushes of sloe, spiny white-thorn. These had blossomed there indeed in the moor's bleak springs long before Post Houses had raised its chimney-pots into the sky. Here, too, flourished a dense drift of dead-nettles—their sour odour haunting the air.

And it was in this forlorn spot that—like Robinson Crusoe before her—Miss Chauncey was suddenly brought to a standstill by the sight of what appeared to be nothing else than a strange footprint in the mould. Nearby the footprint, moreover, showed what might be the impression of a walking-cane or possibly of something stouter and heavier —a crutch. Could she again be deceived? The footprint, it was true, was unlike most human footprints, the heel sunk low, the toe square. Might it be accidental? *Was* it a footprint?

Miss Chauncey glanced up across the bushes toward the house. It looked gaunt and forbidding in the moorland dusk. And she fancied she could see, though the evening light might be deceiving her, the cowering shape of Sam looking out at her from the kitchen-window. To be watched! To be herself spied upon—and watched.

But then of course, Sam was always watching her. What oddity was there in that? Where else would his sprats come from, his cream, his saucer of milk, his bowl of fresh well-water? Nevertheless Miss Chauncey returned to her parlour gravely discomposed.

It was an uncommonly still evening, and as she went from room to room locking the windows, she noticed there was already a moon in the sky. She eyed it with misgiving. And at last bedtime came, and when Sam, as usual after a lick or two had composed himself in his basket, Miss Chauncey, holding the key almost challengingly within view, deliberately locked her bedroom door.

When she awoke next morning Sam was sleeping in his basket as usual, and during the daytime he kept pretty closely to the house. So, too, on the Wednesday and the Thursday. It was not until the following Friday that having occasion to go into an upper bedroom that had no fireplace, and being followed as usual by Sam, Miss Chauncey detected the faint rank smell of soot in the room. No chimney, and a smell of soot! She turned rapidly on her companion; he had already left the room.

And when that afternoon she discovered a black sooty smear upon her own patchwork quilt, she realised not only that her suspicions had been justified, but that for the first time in his life Sam had deliberately laid himself down there in her absence. At this act of sheer defiance, she was no longer so much hurt as exceedingly angry. There was no doubt now. Sam was deliberately defying her. No two companions could share a house on such terms as these. He must be taught a lesson.

That evening in full sight of the creature, having locked her bedroom door, she stuffed a large piece of mattress ticking into the mouth of her chimney and pulled down the register. Having watched these proceedings, Sam rose from his basket, and with an an easy spring, leapt up on the dressing-table. Beyond the window, the moor lay almost as bright as day. Ignoring Miss Chauncey, the creature squatted there steadily and openly staring into the empty skies, for a whole stretch of them was visible from where he sat.

Miss Chauncey proceeded to make her toilet for the night, trying in vain to pretened that she was entirely uninterested in what the animal was at. Faint sounds—not exactly mewings or growlings—but a kind of low inward caterwauling, hardly audible, was proceeding from his throat. But whatever these sounds might mean, Sam himself can have been the

only listener. There was not a sign or movement at the window or in the world without. And then Miss Chauncey promptly drew down the blind. At this Sam at once raised his paw for all the world as if he were about to protest, and then, apparently thinking better of it, he pretended instead that the action had been only for the purpose of commencing his nightly wash.

Long after her candle had been extinguished, Miss Chauncey lay listening. Every stir and movement in the quiet darkness could be clearly followed. First there came a furtive footing and tapping at the register of the fireplace, so closely showing what was happening that Miss Chauncey could positively see in her imagination Sam on the hearth-stone, erecting himself there upon his hind-legs, vainly attempting to push the obstacle back.

This being in vain, he appeared to have dropped back on his fours. Then came a pause. Had he given up his intention? No; now he was at the door, pawing gently scratching. Then a leap, even towards the handle; but one only—the door was locked. Retiring from the door, he now sprang lightly again on to the dressing-table. What now was he at? By covertly raising her head from her pillow, Miss Chauncey could see him with paw thrust out, gently drawing back the blind from the moon-flooded window-pane. And even while she listened and watched, she heard yet again—and yet again—the faint *whssh* as of a wild swan cleaving the air; and then what might have been the cry of a bird, but which to Miss Chauncey's ears resembled a shrill cackle of laughter. At this Sam hastily turned from the window and without the least attempt at concealment pounced clean from the dressing-table on to the lower rail of her bed.

This unmannerly conduct could be ignored no longer. Poor Miss Chauncey raised herself in her sheets, pulled her night-cap a little closer down over her ears, and thrusting out her hand towards the chair beside the bed, struck a match and relit her candle. It was with a real effort that she then slowly turned her head and faced her night-companion. His hair was bristling about his body as if he had had an electric shock. His whiskers stood out at stiff angles with his jaws. He looked at least twice his usual size, and his eyes blazed in his head, as averting his face from her regard he gave vent to a low sustained *Miariou-rou-rou!*

"I say you shall *not*," cried Miss Chauncey at the creature. At the sound of her words, he turned slowly and confronted her. And it seemed that until that moment Miss Chauncey had never actually seen Sam's countenance as in actual fact it really

was. It was not so much the grinning tigerish look it wore, but the sullen assurance upon it of what he wanted and that he meant to get it.

All thought of sleep was out of the question. Miss Chauncey could be obstinate too. The creature seemed to shed an influence on the very air which she could hardly resist. She rose from her bed and thrusting on her slippers made her way to the window. Once more a peculiar inward cry broke out from the bed-rail. She raised the blind and the light of the moon from over the moor swept in upon her little apartment. And when she turned to remonstrate with her pet at his ingratitude, and at all this unseemliness and the deceit of his ways, there was something so menacing and pitiless in his aspect that Miss Chauncey hesitated no more.

"Well, mark me!" she cried in a trembling voice. "Go out of the *door* you shan't. But if you enjoy soot, soot it shall be."

With that she thrust back the register with the poker, and drew down the bundle of ticking with the tongs. And before the fit of coughing caused by the consequent smotheration that followed had ceased, the lithe black shape had sprung from the bed-rail, and with a scramble was into the hearth, over the firebars, up the chimney, and away.

Trembling from head to foot, Miss Chauncey sat down on a cane rocking-chair that stood nearby to reflect what next she must be doing. *Wh-ssh! Wh-ssh!* Again at the window came that mysterious rushing sound, but now the flurrying murmur as of a rocket shooting up with its fiery train of sparks thinning into space, rather than the sound of its descending stick. And then in the hush that followed, there sounded yet again, like a voice from the foot of the garden—a caterwauling piercing and sonorous enough to arouse the sleeping cocks in the Haggurdsdon hen-roosts and for miles around. Out of the distance their chanticleering broke shrill on the night air; to be followed a moment afterwards by the tardy clang of midnight from the church steeple. Then once more silence; utter quiet. Miss Chauncey returned to her bed, but that night she slept no more.

Her mind overflowed with unhappy thoughts. Her faith in Sam was gone. Far worse she had lost faith even in her affection for him. To have wasted that!—all the sprats, all the white-bait in the wide seas were as nothing by comparison. That Sam had wearied of her company was at least beyond question. It shamed her to think how much this meant to here—a mere animal! But she knew what was gone; knew how dull and spiritless in future the day's round would seem—the rising, the housework, the meals, a clean linen collar—the long, slow afternoon, forsaken and companionless! The solitary tea, her candle, prayers, bed—on and on. In what wild company was her cat Sam now? At her own refusal to face that horrid question it was as if she had heard the hollow clanging slam of an immense iron door.

Next morning—still ruminating on these strange events, grieved to the heart at this dreadful rift between herself and one who had been her honest companion of so many years; ashamed, too, that Sam should have had his way with her when she had determined not to allow him to go out during the night—the next morning Miss Chauncey, as if merely to take a little exercise, once again ventured down to the foot of her garden. A faint, blurred mark (such as she had seen on the previous evening) in the black mould of what *might* be a footprint is nothing very much.

But now—in the neglected patch beyond the bushes of white-thorn and bramble—there was no doubt in the world appeared the marks of many. And surely no cats' paw-prints these! Of what use, too, to a cat could a crutch or a staff be? A staff or crutch which—to judge from the impression it had left in the mould—must have been at least as thick as a broomstick.

More disquieted and alarmed than ever over this fresh mystery, Miss Chauncey glanced up and back towards the chimney-pots of the house, clearly and sharply fretted against the morning light of the eastern skies. And she realized what perils even so sure-footed a creature as Sam had faced when he skirred up out of the chimney in his wild effort to emerge into the night. Having thus astonishingly reached the rim of the chimney-pot—the burning stars above and the wilderness of the moor spread out far beneath and around him—he must have leaped from the top of the pot to a narrow brick ledge not three inches wide. Thence on to the peak of the roof and thence down a steep slippery slope of slates to a leaden gutter.

And how then? The thick tod of ivy matting the walls of the house reached hardly more than half-way up: Could Sam actually have plunged from gutter to tod? The very thought of such peril drew Miss Chauncey's steps towards the house again, in the sharpest anxiety to assure herself that he was still in the land of the living.

And lo and behold, when she was but half-way on her journey, she heard a succession of frenzied cries and catcalls in the air from over the moor. Hastily placing a flower-pot by the wall, she stood on tiptoe and peered over. And even now, at this very moment, in full sight across the nearer slope of the moor she descried her Sam, not now in chase of a foolishly trustful visitor, but hotly pursued by what appeared to be the complete rabblement of Haggurdsdon's cats. Sore spent though he showed himself to be, Sam was keeping his distance. Only a few lanky tabby gibs, and what appeared to be a gray-ginger Manx (unless he was an ordinary cat with his tail chopped off) were close behind.

"Sam! Sam!" Miss Chauncey cried, and yet again, "Sam!" but in her excitement and anxiety her foot slipped on the flower-pot and in an instant the feline chase had fallen out of sight. Gathering herself together again, she clutched a long besom or garden broom that was leaning against the wall, and rushed down to the point at which she judged Sam would make his entrance into the garden. She was not mistaken, nor an instant too soon. With a bound he was up and over, and in three seconds the rabble had followed in frenzied pursuit.

What came after Miss Chauncey could never very clearly recall. She could but remember plying her besom with might and main amid the rabble and melée of animals, while Sam, no longer a fugitive, turned on his enemies and fought them cat for cat. None the less, it was by no means an easy victory. And had not the over-fatted cur from the butcher's in Haggurdsdon—which had long since started in pursuit of this congregation of his enemies—had he not at last managed to overtake them, the contest might very well have had a tragic ending. But at the sound of his baying and at sight of the cur's teeth snapping at them as he vainly attempted to surmount the wall, Sam's enemies turned and fled in all directions. And faint and panting, Miss Chauncey was able to fling down her besom and to lean for a brief respite against the trunk of a tree.

At last she opened her eyes again. "Well, Sam," she managed to mutter at last, "we got the best of them, then?"

But to her amazement she found herself uttering these friendly words into a complete vacancy. The creature was nowhere to be seen. His cream disappeared during the day, however, and by an occasional rasping sound Miss Chauncey knew that he once more lay hidden in his dingy resort behind the kindling-wood box. And there she did not disturb him.

Not until tea-time of the following day did Sam reappear. And then—after attending to his hurts—it was merely to sit with face towards the fire, sluggish and sullen and dumb as a dog. It was not Miss Chauncey's "place" to make advances, she thought. She took no notice of the beast except to rub in a little hog's fat on the raw places of his wounds. She was rejoiced to find, however, that he kept steadily to Post Houses for the next few days, though her dismay was reawakened at hearing on the third night a more dismal wailing and wauling than ever from the sloe-bushes, even while Sam himself sat motionless beside the fire. His ears twitched, his fur seemed to bristle; he sneezed or spat, but remained otherwise motionless.

When Mr. Cullings called again, Sam at once hid himself in the coal-cellar, but gradually his manners toward Miss Chauncey began to recover their usual suavity. And within a fortnight after the full-moon, the two of them had almost returned to their old friendly companionship. He was healed, sleek, confident and punctual. No intruder of his species had appeared from Haggurdsdon. The night noises had ceased; Post Homes to all appearances—apart from its strange ugliness—was as peaceful and calm as any other solitary domicile in the United Kingdom.

But alas and alas. With the very first peeping of the crescent moon, Sam's mood and habits began to change again. He mouched about with a sly and furtive eye. And when he fawned on her, purring and clawing, the whole look of him was full of deceit. If Miss Chauncey chanced softly to enter the room wherein he sat, he would at once leap down from the window at which he had been perched as if in the attempt to prove that he had *not* been looking out of it. And once, towards evening, though she was no spy, she could not but pause at the parlour door. She had peeped through its cracks as it stood ajar. And there on the hard sharp back of an old prie-dieu chair that had belonged to her pious great-aunt Jemima, there sat Sam on his hind-quarters. And without the least doubt in the world he was vigorously signalling to some observer outside with his forepaws. Miss Chauncey turned away sick at heart.

From that hour on Sam more and more steadily ignored and flouted his mistress, was openly insolent, shockingly audacious. Mr. Cullings gave her small help indeed. "If I had a cat, m'm, what had manners like that, after all your kindness, fresh fish and all every week, and cream, as I understand, not skim, I'd—I'd give him away."

"To whom?" said Miss Chauncey shortly.

"Well," said the carrier, "I don't know as how I'd much mind to who. Just a home, m'm."

"He seems to have no friends in the Village," said Miss Chauncey in as light a tone as she could manage.

"When they're as black as that, with them saucer eyes, you can never tell," said Mr. Cullings.

"There's that old trollimog what lives in Hogges Bottom. She's got a cat that might be your Sam's twin."

"Indeed no, he has the mange," said Miss Chauncey, loyal to the end. The carrier shrugged his shoulders, climbed into his cart, and bowled away off over the moor. And Miss Chauncey returning into the house, laid the platter of silvery sprats on the table, sat down and burst into tears.

It was, then, in most ways a fortunate thing that the very next morning—three complete days, that is, before the next full-moontide—she received a letter from her sister-in-law in Shanklin, in the Isle of Wight, entreating her to pay them a long visit.

"My dear Emma, you must sometimes be feeling very lonely (it ran), shut up in that great house so far from any neighbours. We often think of you, and particularly these last few days. It's nice to have that Sam of yours for company, but after all, as George says, a pet is only a pet. And we do all think it's high time you took a little holiday with us. I am looking out of my window at this moment. The sea is as calm as a mill-pond, a solemn beautiful blue. The fishing boats are coming in with their brown sails. This is the best time of the year with us, because as it's not yet holy-day-time there are few of those horrid visitors to be seen, and no crowds. George says you *must* come. He joins with me in his love as would Maria if she weren't out shopping, and will meet you at the station in the trap. Emmie is now free of her cough, only whooping when the memory takes her and never sick. And we shall all be looking forward to seeing you in a few days."

At this kindness, and with all her anxieties, Miss Chauncey all but broke down. When the butcher drove up in his cart an hour or two afterwards, he took a telegram for her back to the Village, and on the Monday her box was packed and all that remained was to put Sam in his basket in preparation for the journey. But I am bound to say it took more than the persuasion of his old protectress to accomplish this. Indeed Mr. Cullings had actually to hold the creature with his gloved hands and none too gently, while Miss Chauncey pressed down the lid and pushed the skewer in to hold it close.

"What's done's dumned done!" said the carrier, as he rubbed a pinch of earth into his scratches. "But what I say is, better done forever. Mark my words, m'm!"

Miss Chauncey took a shilling out of her large

leather purse; but made no reply.

Indeed all this trouble proved at last in vain. Thirty miles distant from Haggurdsdon, at Blackmoor Junction, Miss Chauncey had to change trains. Her box and Sam's basket were placed together on the station platform beside half-a-dozen empty milk-cans and some fowls in a crate, and Miss Chauncey went to enquire of the stationmaster to make sure of her platform.

It was the furious panic-stricken cackling of these fowls that brought her hastily back to her belongings, only to find that by hook or by crook Sam had managed to push the skewer of the basket out of its cane loops. The wicker lid yawned open—the basket was empty. Indeed one poor gaping hen, its life fluttering away from its helpless body, was proof not only of Sam's prowess but of his cowardly ferocity.

A few days afterwards, as Miss Chauncey sat in the very room to which her sister-in-law had referred in her invitation, looking over the placid surface of the English Channel, the sun gently shining in the sky, there came a letter from Mr. Cullings. It was in pencil and written upon the back of a baker's bag:

"Dear Madam, i take the libberty of riteing you in referense to the Animall as how i helped put in is bawskit which has cum back returned empty agenn by rail me having okashun to cart sum hop powles from Haggurdsdon late at nite ov Sunday. I seez him squattin at the parlor windy grimasin out at me fit to curdle your blood in your vanes and lights at the upper windies and a yowling and screetching such as i never hopes to hear agen in a Christian lokalety. And that ole wumman from Hogges Botom sitting in the porch mi own vew being that there is no good in the place and the Animall be bewitched. Mr. Flint the fyshmunger agrees with me as how now only last mesures is of any use and as i have said afore i am wiling to take over the house the rent if so be being low and moddrate considering of the bad name it as in these parts around Haggurdsdon. I remain dear madam waitin your orders and oblidge yours truely William Cullings."

To look at Miss Chauncey you might have supposed she was a strong-minded woman. You might have supposed that this uncivil reference to the bad name her family house had won for itself would have mortified her beyond words. Whether or not, she neither showed this letter to her sister-in-law

nor for many days together did she even answer it. Sitting on the Esplanade, and looking out to sea, she brooded on and on in the warm, salt, yet balmy air. It was a distressing problem. But, "No, he must go his own way," she sighed to herself at last; "I have done my best for him."

What is more, Miss Chauncey never returned to Post Houses. She sold it at last, house and garden and for a pitiful sum, to the carrier, Mr. Cullings. By that time Sam has vanished, had been never seen again.

Not that Miss Chauncey was faithless of memory. Whenever the faint swish of a seagull's wing sounded in the air above her head; or the crackling of an ascending rocket for the amusement of the visitors broke the silence of the nearer heavens over the sea; whenever even she became conscious of the rustling frou-frou of her Sunday watered-silk gown as she sallied out to church from the neat little villa she now rented on the Shanklin Esplanade— she never noticed such things without being instantly transported back in imagination to her bedroom at Post Houses, to see again that strange deluded animal, once her Sam, squatting there on her patchwork counterpane, and as it were knitting with his fore-paws the while he stood erect upon his hind.

FIVE EYES

In Hans' old Mill his three black cats
Watch his bins for thieving rats
Whisker and claw, they crouch in the night,
Their five eyes smouldering green and bright:
Squeaks from the flour sacks, squeaks from where
The cold wind stirs on the empty stair,
Squeaking and scampering, everywhere.
Then down they pounce, now in, now out,
At whisking tail, and sniffing snout;
While lean old Hans he snores away
Till peep of light at break of day;
Then up he climbs to his creaking mill,
Out come his cats all grey with meal—
Jekkel, and Jessup, and one-eyed Jill.

James Boswell

1740-1795

LIFE OF
JOHNSON

I never shall forget the indulgence with which he treated Hodge, his cat; for whom he himself used to go out and buy oysters, lest the servants having that trouble should take a dislike to the poor creature. I am, unluckily, one of those who have an antipathy to a cat, so that I am uneasy when in the room with one; and I own, I frequently suffered a good deal from the presence of the same Hodge. I recollect him one day scrambling up Dr. Johnson's breast, apparently with much satisfaction, while my friend, smiling and half-whistling, rubbed down his back, and pulled him by the tail; and when I observed he was a fine cat, saying, 'Why, yes, Sir, but I have had cats whom I liked better than this;' and then, as if perceiving Hodge to be out of countenance, adding, 'but he is a very fine cat, a very fine cat indeed.'

MARIGOLD

She moved through the garden in glory, because
She had very long claws at the end of her paws.
Her back was arched, her tail was high,
A green fire glared in her vivid eye;
And all the Toms, though never so bold,
Quailed at the martial Marigold.

Richard Garnett

ENDOWMENT

But thousands die, without or this or that,
    Die, and endow a college, or a cat.

Alexander Pope

In southern Celebes people try to make rain by carrying a cat tied in a sedan chair thrice round the parched fields, while they drench it with water from bamboo squirts. When the cat begins to miow, they say, "O lord, let rain fall on us!"

The Golden Bough

Index

Acknowledgments

TEXT ACKNOWLEDGMENTS

We gratefully acknowledge permission to reprint the following copyrighted material.

Stephen Vincent Benét: *The King of the Cats* from *The Selected Works of Stephen Vincent Benét Vol. II* edited by Basil Davenport. Copyright 1942 Stephen Vincent Benét. Copyright © 1970 Basil Davenport. Reprinted by permission Holt, Rinehart & Winston, Publishers.

Jorge Luis Borges: *Ficciones* (Excerpt). Copyright © 1962 Grove Press, Inc. Reprinted by permission Grove Press, Inc.

Mikhail Bulgakov: *The Master and Margarita* (Excerpts). Reprinted by permission Grove Press, Inc. Copyright © 1967 by Grove Press, Inc.

Colette: *The Cat* (Excerpt) from *7 By Colette*, translated by Antonia White. Copyright © 1955 by Farrar, Straus, Cudahy, Inc. (now Farrar, Straus & Giroux, Inc.)

Walter de la Mare: *Broomsticks, Five Eyes*. The Literary Trustees of Walter de la Mare, and The Society of Authors as their representative.

T. S. Eliot: *The Naming of Cats, Song of the Jellicles, The Rum Tum Tugger* from *Old Possum's Book of Practical Cats*. Copyright 1939 by T. S. Eliot. Copyright 1967 by Esme Valerie Eliot. Reprinted by permission Harcourt Brace Jovanovich, Inc.

Anne Frank: *The Diary of a Young Girl* (Excerpt). Copyright 1952 by Otto H. Frank. Reprinted by permission Doubleday & Company, Inc.

Paul Gallico: *The Ballad of Tough Tom* from *Honorable Cat*. Copyright © 1972 by Paul Gallico and Mathemata Anstalt. Reprinted by permission Crown Publishers, Inc.

Ernest Hemingway: *Cat in the Rain* from *In Our Time*. Copyright 1925, 1930 Charles Scribner's Sons. Reprinted by permission Charles Scribner's Sons.

Rudyard Kipling: *The Cat that Walked By Himself* from *The Just So Stories*. Reprinted by permission the Executors of the Estate of Mrs. George Bambridge and Doubleday & Company, Inc.

Dilys Laing: *Miao* from *The Collected Poems of Dilys Laing*. Copyright 1967 The Estate of Dily's Laing by David Bennett Laing.

D.H. Lawrence: *Puss-Puss* from *The Complete Poems of D.H. Lawrence* edited by Vivian de Sola Pinto and F. Warren Roberts. Copyright 1964, 1971 by Angelo Ravagli and C. M. Weekley, Executors of The Estate of Frida Lawrence Ravagli. Reprinted by permission The Viking Press.

H. P. Lovecraft: *An Elegy to Oscar* from *Selected Letters Vol. II*. Arkham House Publishers, Inc. Sauk City, Wisconsin.

Don Marquis: *cheerio my deario* from *archy and mehitabel*. Copyright 1927 Doubleday & Company, Inc. Reprinted by permission the publisher.

A. B. Mitford: *The Vampire Cat of Nabéshima* from *Tales of Old Japan*. Charles E. Tuttle Co., Inc. Rutland, Vermont.

Ogden Nash: *The Cat* and *The Kitten* from *Many Long Years Ago*. Copyright 1933 by Ogden Nash. Reprinted by permission Little, Brown and Co.

Alfred Noyes: *Cats and Kings* from *Collected Poems In One Volume*. Copyright 1906, renewed 1934 by Alfred Noyes. Reprinted by permission of J. B. Lippincott Company.

May Swenson: *The Secret in the Cat* from *Poems to Solve*. Copyright 1964 as *His Secret*. May Swenson. Reprinted by permission Charles Scribner's Sons.

James Thurber: *The Pet Department* from *The Thurber Carnival*. Reprinted by permission Helen Thurber (Mrs. James Thurber).

J.R.R. Tolkien: *Cat* from *The Adventures of Tom Bombadil*. Canadian rights courtesy of George Allen & Unwin Ltd.

Mark Twain: *Dick Baker's Cat* (Tom Quartz) from *Roughing It Vol. II*. Reprinted by permission Harper & Row Publishers, Inc. *The Kitten in the Corner Pocket* from *Mark Twain's Letter* edited by Albert Bigelow Paine. Copyright 1917 The Mark Twain Co.

Mark Van Doren: *Midwife Cat* from *Collected and New Poems 1924-1963*. Copyright 1963 Mark Van Doren. Reprinted by permission Farrar, Straus & Giroux, Inc.

Tennessee Williams: *The Malediction* (Excerpt) from *One Arm & Other Stories*. Copyright 1948 Tennessee Williams. Reprinted by permission New Directions Publishing Corp.

William Carlos Williams: *Poem* from *Collected Earlier Poems*. Copyright 1938 New Directions Publishing Corp. Reprinted by permission New Directions Publishing Corp.

P.G. Wodehouse: *The Story of Webster* from *Mulliner Nights*. Reprinted by permission of the author and the author's agents, Scott Meredith Literary Agency, Inc., 845 Third Ave. N.Y. 10022.

W. B. Yeats: *The Cat and the Moon* from *Collected Poems*. Copyright 1919 MacMillan Publishing Co., Inc. Renewed 1947 Bertha Georgie Yeats. *A Vision* (Excerpt). Copyright 1937 W. B. Yeats, renewed 1965 Bertha Georgie Yeats and Anne Butler Yeats. Reprinted by permission MacMillan Publishing Co., Inc.

ART ACKNOWLEDGMENTS

We gratefully acknowledge permission to reproduce the following material.

Marc Chagall (1889-   ) *Paris Through the Window*. The Solomon R. Guggenheim Museum, New York. Page 74-75

Leonardo da Vinci (1452-1519) *Sketches of Cats*. Royal Library, Windsor Castle. Copyright Reserved. Reproduced by permission Her Majesty the Queen. Page 10

Eugène Delacroix (1798-1863) *Head of Cat*. Musée du Louvre, Paris. Arch Phot. Paris/S.P.A.D.E.M. Page 57

Theodore Géricault (1701-1824) *White Cat*. Ny Carlsberg Glyptotek, Copenhagen. *Studies of a Striped Cat*. Fogg Art Museum, Harvard University, Cambridge. *Studies of a Striped Cat*. (Detail). Page 2-3, 95, (front flap)

J.A.D. Ingres (1780-1867) *Madame Ingres' Kitten Asleep in her Arms*. Musée Ingres, Montauban, France. Page 1

Nadar (1820-1910) *Caricature of Theóphile Gautier*. Arch Phot. Paris/S.P.A.D.E.M. Page 29

Jean Baptiste Oudry (1686-1755) *Kittens*. Fitzwilliam Museum, Cambridge. *Study of a Cat*. Musée D'Histoire, Paris. Arch Phot. Paris/S.P.A.D.E.M. Page 36, 47

Auguste Renoir (1841-1919) *Woman with a Cat*. National Gallery of Art, Washington. Gift of Mr. and Mrs. Benjamin E. Levy 1950. Page 77

Joseph Whiting Stock (19th century) *Mary Jane Smith, aged 2 yrs. 4 mos.* Abby Aldrich Rockefeller Folk Art Collection, Williamsburg, Va. Page 37

Giovanni Battista Tiepolo (1692-1770) *Two Sleeping Cats*. Victoria and Albert Museum, London. Page 18

Cornelius Visscher (1619?-1662) *Cat*. Museum Boymans-van Beuningen, Rotterdam. Page 31

Andrew Wyeth (1917-   ) *Miss Olson and a Kitten, 1952*. Private Collection. Page 31

Artist Unknown (c. 1840) French Wallpaper Fireboard. Cooper-Hewitt Museum, New York, The Smithsonian's National Museum of Design. Page 60-61

Back Cover: Artist Unknown (19th century) *Lydia and Tabitha*. Abby Aldrich Rockefeller Folk Art Collection, Williamsburg, Va